Log Cabin Escape.
The Sequel

"He led me beside the still waters."

**A Christian based Novel
by
Arnold Kropp**

This is a work of fiction. Names, characters, businesses, places, events, locales, and incidents are either the products of the author's imagination or used in a fictitious manner. Any resemblance to actual persons, living or dead, or actual events is purely coincidental.

The use of the name of Jesus and all references to God are spiritually intended.

Scripture references are from the AKJV.

Copyright   Arnold Kropp. 2022

All rights reserved.

Log Cabin Escape, The Sequel

Author : Kropp, Arnold
ISBN : 9780578380858

E-pub; 9780578380865

Yes, I dedicate this to all my grandsons.

And, to those faithful ones of the novel idea and the critical link group: Rita and the others who've suggested changes, and corrected my grammatical mishaps.

Thank you. Thank you.

20 And God said, Let the waters bring forth abundantly the moving creature that hath life, and fowl that may fly above the earth in the open firmament of heaven.

21 And God created great whales, and every living creature that moveth, which the waters brought forth abundantly, after their kind, and every winged fowl after his kind: and God saw that it was good.

22 And God blessed them, saying, Be fruitful, and multiply, and fill the waters in the seas, and let fowl multiply in the earth.

23 And the evening and the morning were the fifth day.

24 And God said, Let the earth bring forth the living creature after his kind, cattle, and creeping thing, and beast of the earth after his kind: and it was so.

25 And God made the beast of the earth after his kind, and cattle after their kind, and every thing that creepeth upon the earth after his kind: and God saw that it was good.

Genesis 1: 20-25 (AKJV}

Log Cabin Escape.
The Sequel

"He led me beside the still waters."

One

"Ah, King, come here!" Samuel rubs behind his playful German Shepherd's ears, whose front paws pull on the blanket covering Samuel. "Okay, time to go," he says as he throws the cover to his right. King leads him to the front door, and King runs toward the Gazebo.

"Good morning, Monday," Samuel tells the air. He is at the sink, pumping water into the coffee pot. The Coleman stove is on. He strikes a match to a crumbled piece of paper under some sliced bark and adds three pieces of wood into the cast iron stove to help warm the cabin. As the coffee brews, he gets the fireplace burning. He peels a banana and steps outside to feel the fresh air.

Hmm? More snow overnight.

King comes running to the deck with the Frisbee in his jaw. Samuel throws it toward the pier. King takes off. Samuel goes back inside. He dons a hooded sweatshirt, a jacket, and boots and then pours a cup of black coffee, and he

"Now, King, you know we're not going to play this all morning, so one more, and that's it." He throws the Frisbee behind the gazebo.

He leans back in the rocker, resting his head on the little pillow placed over the wood header. He begins to think of the future event in his life. It's eleven days to Thanksgiving when he and Francinea plan to announce their engagement to their friends in this cabin. *Man, I've got to get this place cleaned up and ready for that, but how? What else should I do? The barn? The gazebo? How many will come? Harry and Meredith. Gene and his wife. George and his wife. The sheriff and his wife. Francinea's medical partner and his wife. That's twelve, counting her and me. Will Francinea want anyone else? The church pastor? Harry and Meredith may want the youth pastor. Who else? Now we're up to possibly sixteen. How about the Vet? Will they all be able to get away from their family traditions on Thanksgiving evening? Ah, too many questions. Too much of this.*

"Lord, lead the way and remove these unknowns."

After a sip of coffee, Samuel leans over and rubs Kings' neck and down his side. He sips more coffee and then heads over to the barn. He grabs a shovel, a clipper, a rake, a towel, and a bucket and carries them to the gazebo as King takes off into the woods. Samuel starts to clip back the vines hanging over the sides and throws them into a pile. He flips the cushions on the bench, wipes the wood bench clean, and leans the soft cushions against the back. He sweeps the fallen leaves into a pile next to the cut vines. He sweeps leaves away from the path to the porch and the pier. *Ah, I wish I could put a set of lights around this.*

King trots out of the woods, stops, and rubs his nose back and forth through the snow covering the browned grass. He does it again and again, then stops at the feet of his master.

"Oh, you stink. You didn't, did you?" Samuel puts his glove over his nose and mouth. "Yes, you did. Was it fun?" He walks to the barn, and King follows him inside. "No, you are not going into the cabin smelling like that." He puts his hand in front of the dog's nose, "Stay!"

Samuel quickly closes the barn door leaving King inside. In the cabin, he pumps water into a large pot and places it on the stovetop to warm while he gets two buckets, some soap, and brushes. *Is this enough, or do I need other cleansing items?* "Oh, yes, shampoo. Some lavender scent ought to do it." He pours the warmed water into one of the buckets and pumps more water to heat. He dumps some dishwater soap into the bucket and some shampoo, mixes it well, as another bucket of water warms up a bit. *I saw some plastic gloves in this closet.* Sam opens a plastic container searching for the gloves.

"Okay." Samuel carries the two buckets, brush, and a towel out to the barn. He slides open the barn door. King jumps up to put his paws on Sam, who moves to deflect those and his nose. Samuel buckles the leash onto his collar and ties the end to a hook on the wall. He ties a rope to the collar and the end to a board on the opposite wall to restrain his pet. He pours some of the soapy water over the dog's head, and King licks the soapy water. "No! Stop it!"

He drenches the dog and brushes the solution into the hairs and over the body with one hand as the other hand slowly rubs the soapy water again and again. "Gads King, Quit it!" He slowly pours the clear water over the dog. He wraps the towel around his pet to dry him off. *Will that do it?* He wonders as King shakes his body, spraying the water toward Samuel.

He leaves his pet in the barn and walks to the cabin, where he takes the truck keys, puts a clean jacket, sweatshirt, and jeans into a sack, and carries it to the passenger seat of the truck. He unties the rope and leash and leads King up onto the back of the pickup. He removes the plastic gloves, inserts the key, starts the engine, and drives off. Ten minutes later, Samuel parks the truck in front of the veterinarian's office.

"My dog got sprayed by a skunk. I sure hope you can clean that off." Samuel tells the lady at the window. "I tried but felt it wouldn't be good enough."

The office door opens. "Hey, Samuel. How are you? King in trouble again? Is it King you want us to clean or you?"

"Funny. Doc, I tried, but."

"Bring him in, and we'll take care of it for you. King doing okay otherwise?

"Oh, yes. He's probably cold now from riding in the bed of the truck. I tried to dry the soapy water off, but . . ."

"Hey, we'll take him," The vet interrupts.

After handing King's leash to the vet, Samuel follows them into the backroom. He watches as the vet and the lady in white protective clothing, hoods, and face masks prepare to clean King.

"Sam, this is going to take a while to remove all that smell thoroughly, so if you'd like to go somewhere, you can."

"Thanks. Will that smell linger on after everything you do?"

"It may have to be done again in a few hours." The Vet answers, "Considering your cabin, he needs a warmer atmosphere, so it may be better if you let King stay the night."

"Thanks, Doc. What time tomorrow?"

"About noon or a bit after. If there's any odor left in the morning, we'll be able to handle it then. Sometimes the smell will linger awhile. And, with King's fur, it most likely will take two or more washings.

"Doc, you're a blessing. Is there any chance that you could come to the cabin Thanksgiving evening, say about six for dessert and . . .well, an announcement? I'm having a few others over for that special day to celebrate this nation's great beginning. Meredith and her mother will be there."

"Sam, that sounds great. I'll discuss it with my wife and kids."

"Thanks, Doc. I hope you can make it. But now, I've got to go to the laundromat. I'll pick him up tomorrow after lunch," Samuel says. He points to King. "Now, King, be a good doggie." He turns, leaves the office, and walks out to his truck.

Inside the laundromat, Samuel quickly carries the sack of clean clothes into the restroom. He changes, comes out, and selects a machine to throw the smelly garments inside. Scanning the area, he notices that the three customers have their eyes on him rather than the magazines they're holding. *Gads, could they have smelled me as I walked in?*

A lady attendant approaches him. "Now, sir, to get rid of that skunk smell, we've got a special solution you should use."

"Thanks," Samuel replies. "I was wondering about that. Sorry to disturb your pleasant atmosphere here. My dog got it. The vet is taking care of that. So, I'm here to get it off me."

"I've got a spray for our inside area too. And you can use it for the car as your clothes wash."

"Oh, thank you. I'm Samuel Guardyall," shaking hands with this sweet lady.

"Joyce Ripper," she replies. "Yes, I've heard about you moving into that cabin in the woods. You met my husband, Jack, in the diner awhile back."

"Oh, yes. We only talked briefly," Samuel replies. "He said you were heading south for the winter."

"We were, and are, but not until after Thanksgiving. Kids are coming for a visit. Our two sons, their wives, and our five grandkids are driving up from Denver, so we put it off a few weeks."

"That sounds wonderful. The soap! I should get started."

"Yes, I'll be right back." She turns and enters the private area.

Joyce helps Samuel choose the right setting and scatters the detergent on top of his clothes. He thanks her and goes out to spray down the truck bed and the insides. He returns the can of spray to Joyce. "I'd be glad to spray the air inside here for you. Just tell me how much and where. Your husband told me that the Fish and Wildlife Agency said they did not need him anymore. How long had he worked as one of the forest rangers?"

"Thirty-five years," Joyce answers. "Mr. Guardyall, your grandmother was a fantastic lady. I learned much from her at those cooking classes she held in the cabin and the library. Did your dog kill the skunk, or just got sprayed?"

"I hadn't thought of that. All I wanted was to get rid of the smell, and . . . well . . . he did not have it when he approached."

"I'll never forget the demonstration she had about preparing and cooking a skunk."

"What? People eat skunks?"

"Oh, yes. Your grandmother once demonstrated the cleaning and the preparations for a skunk stew."

"I'm going to take another look through those recipes she left me. But, oooh, just the thought of it drives me off the wall."

The washing machine bell rings. He pulls the wet-washed Jacket, sweatshirt, and jeans out, smells them, and throws them in a dryer. "Joyce, that solution with baking soda seemed to have worked. Thanks."

"No problem. Samuel, I'm sure Jack would be pleased to have you over for dinner someday, or even better yet, we'd welcome you to join us for Thanksgiving."

"Thanks. But I've got plans for Thanksgiving."

"How about this Friday evening, then?"

"I think I could make that. Would it be okay if I brought a friend? She's a doctor here."

"Would that be Mrs. Ingersall? She treated Jack for a bruised shoulder about a month ago."

"Yes. That's her. I cut my leg open instead of cutting the wood, and she was the one who stitched it. And we've become friends."

"Let's do it—Friday evening at about seven. Here, I'll write our address down for you. Samuel, your skunk episode has made my day."

"Thanks, but you made my day too. To think I'd have such a sweet time after this fiasco with King. God is wonderful with these surprises."

Sam gets his clothes from the dryer and tells Susan, "Friday evening. Thanks so much." Sam leaves the laundromat in his cleaned clothes and heads to the diner for a late lunch.

"Hey, Samuel! Where have you been?" Joanna states as he selects a booth.

"I came to see if you wanted to pick my bone again."

"You are full of it, aren't you? Your happy face is shining. So, what's going on?"

"Ah, Joanna, I thought I'd come here and let you know my dog got sprayed by a skunk and to see if you could prepare a skunk stew for me?"

"Okay, I got it. Nothing's going on, so you're here to harass me or follow me as I shoot another deer so that you can bury it."

"Coffee and one of those burgers, the single, not the triple, and the side of onion rings."

"Be right back with the coffee." Her gum-chewing intensifies as she leaves the booth.

Samuel peers around the diner to see if he recognizes anyone. Nope, all kind of quiet this early afternoon.

"Samuel," Joanna says as she sets the cup of coffee and napkin in front of him. "I've been hearing things about you and the doctor."

"What? Me and Dr. Josen?"

"No, not him. His partner, Francinea."

"What? The rumor is that she's the one who stitched up my leg? Yes, she did that, and I've seen her in her office. Is that the top rumor of the week?"

"Something romantic. Are you two getting it on in that cabin of yours."

"Now, Joanna, you know me better than that. Who's been telling you this?"

"See that couple over there?" She turns to look at the couple at the counter. "They're here visiting from Indianapolis."

Samuel carefully looks at the lady and gentleman, who appear to be in their fifties. "So? What did they say?"

Joanna sits down opposite him in the booth, leans over, and softly tells Sam that they asked her about some guy named Samuel, who is going to marry their friend Francinea. Said they came up here to help her celebrate the good news. "They asked about you. Is it true that you two are engaged?"

"Joanna, I appreciate you. You've taught me a bunch since I've been here, and God only knows what's in my future. My sandwich?"

"Oh. Yes, it must be ready." Joanna replies and leaves to get the burger and onion rings. "Enjoy it, and it was good to see you today. Sorry about your dog. But dang it, don't stay away too long."

"Joanna, please do not say anything to anybody about our engagement. Yes, it's true, and you're the first in town to hear, so please do not, okay?"

"Sam, my lips are sealed. It's fantastic, and the two of you deserve each other. Thanks for the real update. I promise on my Girl Scout oath not to say anything." Joanna swipes her lips with her forefinger.

"Thanks, Joanna. I ought to introduce myself to that couple."

Joanna replies, "Yes, come. I'll introduce you."

"Deal." Samuel follows Joanna, who carries his food and coffee to the counter. She sets the plate and coffee down next to the couple.

"Hey, you asked about a guy named Samuel," Joanna tells the couple. "Here, he is. Samuel Guardyall. He came in a few minutes ago. And, welcome to Prairieville. The meals are on me today. So, again, welcome."

"Hi, I'm Mark Bannister, and my wife, Susan."

"Greetings," Sam says. "Why did you ask about me?"

"We're old friends with Francinea," Susan says. "We've wanted to visit her since that big move of hers, and well, here we are. She called and informed us that she got engaged. And you're it."

"Yes. I'm the lucky one. I moved here from Shelbyville six or seven months ago to a log cabin my grandparents lived in for their ninety-some years. What a difference it's been. This small-town life has been fascinating, along with having to learn to adjust to life without electricity. God has been so good, helping me to like waking up to a cold floor. How long have you known Fran?"

"Fran and I have been friends since our high school days," Susan informs. "I'm a nurse, but she managed to become a doctor. I've wanted to visit before this to see how she's adjusting, but we couldn't get away until now. We just arrived an hour ago wanting to surprise her today, but she's at that hospital. So, this evening we will."

Mark says, "So Samuel, what are your plans?"

"My plans? Well, this evening, I planned to tell her of my deal with a skunk this morning, but this is your turn, so I'll hold off."

"No, about the engagement, the marriage," Susan interjects.

Sam says, "well, we've kept it a secret so far. She wanted to wait until Thanksgiving and do that in the cabin. Fran doesn't know you were coming?"

"Not exactly when," Susan answers.

Looking at the couple, Sam says, "Well, another great surprise today. When you see Fran, I pray she's excited as you are, and I wish I had a camera to snap a shot of her face when she sees you. She has a beautiful home just a bit north of here. A beautiful setting."

Mark says, "Got it pegged in Maps."

"If you don't mind, I'd like to pray for you, your visit, and a safe return home."

Sam leans over and takes a hand from Mark and Susan, bows his head, and prays loud enough for them to hear. "Thank You, Lord, for today and your surprises, and now for this couple. That you keep them safe and a wonderful time renewing friendships. Bless them in all they do. Amen. Oh, and also, thanks for the help with my dog. For Joyce's help too, and well, Lord, You know. Thanks be to the great I Am."

"Thank you," Susan says.

"Well, I hate to leave, but I've got work to do cleaning that smell out of my barn and cabin before Thanksgiving. Bless you, this evening." Samuel then asks, "How long will you be staying?"

"We've got to head back Thursday. It's a two day trip," Susan moans.

"Hey, yes. It's still early afternoon, so you've got several hours till Fran gets home. So, why don't you come to see the cabin now? You'll see where she's agreed to live after the wedding. Not much else to do around town."

They look at each other, at the watch, and nod, "Sure, let's do it, we got time." Susan answers.

"Follow me. A short drive," Samuel says, and they all leave the diner.

Samuel parks his truck near the cabin porch. He quickly goes to the driver's side of Mark and Susan's car behind his truck. "Sorry, I hadn't thought this through, but that skunk smell may be in the cabin, so we better not go in."

"Oh, Sam, the setting of it all is wonderful," Susan says. "Mark and I would be overwhelmed to find a place like this for a vacation."

"How's the lake for fishing?" Mark asks.

"The fishing is great. A couple of streams feed the lake from the surrounding hills, and another stream is going out on the far end to the south. So, it's continually refreshed."

Mark then says, "I've read stories about the fish and wildlife agencies keeping powerboats off their lakes."

'Yeah," Samuel replies. "They've done that here. All I can use is that rowboat down there by the pier." He points to it. "They'd like to take over this cabin since the national forest surrounds my acreage. So, I cannot change anything. I must leave it as it was when they declared the area as a national forest. Are you warm enough to take a short walk? I could show you my favorite place to sit and contemplate. About five minutes, that's all."

Mark looks at Susan. "Sure. The scenery is like a national geographic magazine story. No wonder Fran has fallen in love with this."

Samuel leads them toward the lake and then into the woods for the short walk to the stream, where a camp chair faces the lakeside view of the rolling hills stretching into snow-capped mountains.

"Well, this is it. My dog has kept me company, but soon I'll have Fran to take away some of that loneliness." They walk back to their car while thanking Sam for the brief tour of the area.

"As I said before," Susan says. "it's beautiful, Sam, and now I know why Fran has agreed to your proposal. If Mark had a place like this, I would have fallen for him a lot sooner."

"Good day then, and thanks again," Sam says. He bids them a happy reunion. And they drive off.

Two

Right after they leave midafternoon, Samuel sprays down the barn, the spot where he restrained King, the entrance, and to be sure it's clear of the odor, and he sprays everything once more.

"Oh, thank You, Lord, for the help you sent my way today."

Yuck! Skunks! Why are they here, Lord? How did Noah handle skunks in that boat?

Leaving the barn and entering the cabin, the first thing Sam does is to make a pot of coffee. While it's brewing, Samuel grabs the lavender spray can. He points the mist around the entrance, the path to his bed area, the dresser, the closet, and the handle gets a double squirt. He then steps around the cabin, sniffing as he goes. "Okay, and now to start cleaning everything else."

He looks up to the rafters. "Oh, the dust." He mumbles. For the next hour, Samuel intently dusts and wipes down the beams. He leaves the accessible areas' details to another time.

"No King until tomorrow, so time for a just me walk into these woods." *"So,"* he wonders, *"where was it that King got sprayed?"* He's trying to follow the dogs' footprints, but nothing so far. He leaves footsteps in the fresh snow, periodically throwing a snowball. Samuel keeps to the path and comes to the visible road area. He continues his trek, making his way down the entrance and back to the cabin. He pours himself a fresh hot, steaming cup of coffee and reclines back on the rocker after brushing off the flecks of snow.

"Thank You, Lord, for this peace," and then he hears a rumble coming down the entrance path, headlights flashing, and three quick honks.

"Francinea! What a surprise!"

"Good evening. It is, isn't it, or am I disturbing your peace?" Francinea asks.

He pulls her in for a hug and a quick kiss. Holding her tight, he whispers, "Ah, it's great to see you. Thanks."

She pushes herself away and states, "What's that smell? Have you changed your deodorant?"

"No!" Sam replies. "I've changed my coffee. Is it that bad?"

"It's not the coffee. Something like lavender. That's not like you to put that on. Who you trying to impress? Well, anyway, hon, I got some time off, and here I am. I stopped to let you know about a call I got a few days ago. I almost told you yesterday after church, but we were interrupted. I suspect some friends from home will be coming up for a few days' visit. Not exactly sure when, but when they do, I want them to see this cabin and the area. I told her of our engagement, so she wants to get to know you."

"No, kidding," Sam answers. "Oh, let me get you some coffee first." He gets off the rocker and opens the door for Francinea.

Inside, she immediately sniffs the scent of lavender and says, "Gads, Samuel, why is that lavender odor so dominant."

"Oh, that's a long story," he replies as he hands her a cup of coffee. "let's sit by the fireplace."

"Okay, you want to know why. King got sprayed by a skunk this morning. I took him to the vet, so he'll be fine in a few days. Then I came back here and started cleaning some of that odor I left inside. Don't you like lavender?"

"Wow. No, really, not that much. What a morning you've had. Back to these friends of mine. When they get here, we'll set a time so that you can be at you're best in Sunday garb without lavender."

"Sunday garb? What's that?" Samuel teases.

"Oh, that's when you put on a suit and tie, matching socks, polished shoes, deodorant, shaved, and nicely combed hair."

Samuel intensely peers into her eyes. "Huh? No pants? Sure, that would be interesting. Yeah! I might do that if, at the wedding, I can wear my daily romp through the woods or fishing attire?"

"Oh, Samuel, will you ever let me have a one up on you? But just wait. I'll get ya!" She playfully pokes him in the stomach, and he gets off the couch, turns to step away for a moment, looks back, and then raises his arms, surrendering. *How do I do this? They want it to be a surprise, and If I tell Francinea about meeting them at the diner, It'll ruin that surprise this evening. What do I say? I can't lie to her.*

"I give. Now tell me more about these friends of yours you expect any day." He sits back on the couch, his leg up, with the knee resting on the cushion and his arm stretched out on the back of the sofa for a good view into her eyes.

"Oh," Francinea begins, "Susan and I were close all through high school." She details their enjoyment of walks through the woods while talking about boys. "We remained friends after college and continued those walks. She's a nurse. Now, Mark, her husband, is kind of quiet. He writes a column for the Weekly Times and coaches the high school baseball team. When Jerome was home, they played golf. Samuel, do you have any of your stew left over? Let's eat, and I can relax here for the rest of the evening. Meredith has a shift now at the Vet's office, so there's no need for me to go home."

"Oh," Sam lightly says, thinking about her friends wanting to surprise her as she gets home from work.

"Samuel, what is it? Why the hesitation?"

"Ah, the stew? Nothing left."

"Fix me something else then. Surely, with all your grandmother's recipes, we can put some kind of dinner together."

Lord, how can I do this without upsetting her and ruining the surprise? Samuel silently prays.

"You say Meredith is working this evening? King's at the Vet office. Then, let's go to your house, and we can spend the evening there. Nice and warm and comfortable."

"We could do that. But I wanted to spend another evening here next to this fireplace. You know, get used to this cabin life some more."

"Yes, and I'm thrilled that you did—a great surprise. I was gonna stop by your home this evening after checking on King.

"You want to check on King? Let's go then, and I'll fix you a meal you won't forget."

"I'll take the truck and see you after I stop to see how King is responding. And, no suit and tie as I sold them all before moving here."

"Take your time then, but not too long."

Sam leans over and pulls her in close. He whispers in her ear, "Ah, Thank you, Lord, for bringing this wonderful, beautiful gal into my life." Their lips meet and move in love.

Sam helps her off the couch, and they walk arm in arm to the door. They hug and kiss again, and she steps out onto the porch. Looking back, she says, "No more than half an hour. Okay? I'll leave the door open, so just come on in."

On the porch, he watches her drive around the bend. Back inside the cabin, Sam looks at his watch seeing the time at 5:20. *Hmm? It'll take her ten to fifteen minutes to get home. Will Mark and Susan get there before I do? If I don't see Mark's car, should I drive around the block and wait? Park down the street, and when I see them stopping at the house, wait ten minutes?*

Sam walks into the vet's office, immediately seeing Meredith through the office window sitting on the desktop chatting with the clerk. "Hey, Meredith," he says. "Doing an evening shift, eh? How's King?"

"Hi, Samuel. He's okay. The smell is almost gone. They'll do another cleansing in the morning." She presses a button. The door buzzes. "Go on in and see." Sam pulls the door open and walks down the hallway to the pen area.

"King, my boy."

"Woof, woof, woof." King paws the wires. Sam slides a few fingers through the wires to get them licked on by King. "Ah, you don't smell like a skunk anymore. That's good." The nails of the dog's paw pull on the wires along with those barks. Sam reaches in his pocket and puts a treat up for the dog to see. King smells and barks as Sam hands it to him through the wire.

Meredith approaches and says, "King will be back to normal tomorrow. Now, Samuel, I've wanted to let you know that Mom has been like a different person since your proposal. It's like the old days. We went for a walk in the woods, and that's when she told me. So, welcome, and congratulations."

Sam then tells her, "Thanks, Meredith. Your mother did not want to disturb your excitement and thought she'd hold off telling you. Hmm? But I guess she did. Let's go somewhere where we can talk openly."

Meredith leads him to a separate room. "Here," she says and closes the door behind her.

Seated comfortably inside the room, Sam says, "And, congratulations for you too. I felt that Harry would, but not until after graduation. I could already sense that this is how it would develop when he stopped that snowy day for you to see the cabin. Did your mother say anything about making the announcements on Thanksgiving?"

"I'm having a tough time keeping it quiet until then. My friends keep asking me what's going on, and it's hard not to say anything. So, the sooner we do it, the better, but we're still discussing it. This is where we're at now. The last day of school before the Christmas break. New Years Day, a party at Harry's. I'm excited for mom and, ah, really don't want to disturb her joy. Thanksgiving would be nice, but it's all your friends, and, well, you know, the difference in ages do make a difference. I think my school friends would feel uncomfortable there among all those adults."

"You got a good point there. Have you discussed this with your mother? What does she say?"

"No, I haven't."

"Why not?"

"Ah, she's so excited. Most of the time, I feel like I'm just a daughter being told things." She pauses and then adds. "Samuel, you're so easy to talk to, like a priest behind the curtain."

"Thanks, but your mother is there for you. Open up, and you may be surprised. Hey, let me pray for you right this minute." He reaches for her hand and kneels. "Father God, we are looking to you to direct Meredith and her path. Speak to her and Harry and guide them in an open approach to her mother to let it all out. You have healed Francinea of the past sorrows. Now heal Meredith in the same loving way. She's excited about the coming events in her life. Direct all that. We love you, Lord. Amen"

"Thank you," Meredith responds, wiping her cheeks.

"God has this under control, so relax, and be yourself. You've got a talent and abilities that will bless many. Your mother is fixing me a dinner that I'll never forget. Thanks again for your help with King."

Sam drives his pickup to Francinea's neighborhood. Approaching her home, he sees Mark and Susan's vehicle parked in front of the mailbox. *Ah, they're here.* Sam pulls into the driveway, gets out, and slowly walks to the front door finding it open. He knocks and enters her home. Francinea runs to greet him.

"Samuel, they're here." She excitedly says.

"Who?" he says.

"My friends from home. They were sitting in the car, waiting for me to arrive." She grabs his arm and pulls him down the hallway to the living room. As they enter the room, Samuel shakes his head back and forth, hoping they will understand his desire to pretend they haven't met. "Mark and Susan, this is Samuel." Mark stands to shake Sam's hand, and then Sam reaches over to shake Susans' hand.

"Well, it's great to see you. Fran told me that you might come. So, welcome, And I can see that she is flowing with joy. The timing of your visit is perfect."

"Samuel, you're ten minutes late. Is anything wrong with King?"

"No, King is fine," he answers and then looks toward Mark and Susan, comfortably seated on the couch. He tells them that King, his dog, a German Shepherd, got sprayed by a skunk. "So, how was your trip? Did you like going through that Denver and Boulder traffic?"

"Ah, we're used to that. No problem," Mark replies.

"Honey," Francinea says. "I haven't cooked a thing, so we're waiting for pizza delivery. So, sit and get acquainted." He and Francinea relax in the cushioned chairs facing the long couch. "I told you a little about them, but they want to know more about my future husband."

Susan says, "You're living in an old log cabin surrounded by this forest. That must have been a hard adjustment."

"It was. But arriving in late spring enabled me to learn through the summer, making it easier." Sam pauses. He looks down at his hands and then at Susan and Mark, thinking of the information he's holding back from Francinea. *This ain't right. She should know we've already met.*

He turns and peers into the eyes of his bride-to-be. He reaches for her hand. "Francinea, I've got a confession to make. You should know. After dropping King off this morning, I stopped at the diner, and Joanna pointed to Mark and Susan at the counter. So, we've already met. I'm sorry to have led you on."

"What?" She exclaims. "You've already met?" She withdraws her hand from his. "Susan already told me they met you in the diner. So there. And here I was wondering, thinking about a way to get you back for not telling me. I was hoping you'd not mention it, and then I could pounce on you. Thanks, but you owe me one. Just wait. But why didn't you tell me this afternoon?" Francinea asks.

"At the time, I thought it'd spoil the joy in your anticipation. Thinking about it now, that was well—a selfish motive of mine, because you'd probably left right away while I was enjoying your company."

"Yep," Susan then says. "You two deserve each other. Fran, I couldn't be happier for you. Samuel, Fran was like that in school, always pulling something on me and then confessing. It went buzzing over my head the first few times, but then I learned and started the same with her. It became a game."

"Yeah, Sue, you were good at it too," Francinea replies. " Now, where's that pizza. I'm ready to eat. Into the kitchen with me, Sue, and we'll get the table set. Let the boys talk."

"Sam," Mark begins. "Fran said she has agreed to move into that cabin of yours. The area is amazing, but we'd sure like to see the inside of it."

"Of course. No problem. If Francinea can get time off, she can drive you out tomorrow. Hey Fran," Sam raises his voice calling to her in the kitchen around the corner.

She peeks around the corner. "Yes, what is it?"

"Can you get some time off tomorrow? They'd like to see the cabin."

"I'll make a call in the morning. But, yes. I believe I could."

"Okay. Lunchtime would be great, and I could have a skunk stew for us all."

"Ah, forget it, Francinea replies. "We'll bring three of Joanna's burger sandwiches and watch you eat the stew." She then turns back into the kitchen.

"Mark, when I lived in Shelbyville, I had season tickets for the Colt games. How are they doing this year?"

"Not that well. Three and six, so far. But I don't care much about football anymore. Baseball is my sport. Still coaching high school baseball. When I can, Sue and I'll drive to Chicago to watch the Cubs."

"When I first moved here, I thought I'd miss all that. But now that I've adjusted to a life without, I couldn't care less. Waking through the woods or just sitting by the lake is what has captivated me. It's been magical viewing the wonders of nature and pondering how it all came to be. That's become so much better than being entertained by twenty-two guys bumping heads over a ball."

"I can only imagine being without all that. I'd love it for a weekend, a vacation, but all the time. No. Couldn't do it."

"I had my doubts too. The notes my grandfather left have helped a great deal to get over the loneliness of being without, well, continual contact with others, along with the simple thing like a cell phone connecting me with the world. And I've managed to make it for seven months without it. You could do it."

"Because you asked how the Colts are doing tells me you still have an interest in that outside world."

Samuel does not immediately respond; his eyes move back and forth from Mark to his fingers, and then tells Mark, "Yeah, I mentioned the cell phone too. Of course, these tidbits of technology, the media, sports, and movies stream across my mind now and then. Sure, I miss them. But not to the point that I want to get back into it full-time. And the feds help too by requiring the cabin be left as it was. Yes, I cannot connect to the power grid."

Francinea peeks around the corner to tell Sam and Mark that dinner is ready. "Come and get it."

"Hang on a minute." Samuel hollers back. He looks back at Mark, who is beginning to get up. "Mark, back in Shelbyville, I assumed that because I was a member of a church and faithfully attended the services, I was a Christian. But that was in name only. In reality, I had not fully understood what Jesus had done, and now, I will not return to that previous life. There. It's final, and that's how I feel about this lifestyle I've embraced, and Fran has agreed to join me." He and Mark then enter the kitchen/dining room and sit at their assigned seats.

"Come on guys, sit; your pizza is ready," Francinea announces.

Samuel holds his hands open above the table. The four of them grab hold while Samuel offers a quick blessing. And then Francinea stands and places two pizza slices on each plate. "Sam, the one on the left is a special one for you."

"Oh," he replies. "That must be part of the dinner I'd never forget."

"Yes," Francinea replies. "Enjoy it."

Sam bends his head to see up close the slice and replies, "It smells like lavender."

"Yee gads, you can smell after all you did yesterday," Francinea claims.

"Fran, don't you and Sam ever have serious conversations?" Susan quirks.

"Sure we do, but we also enjoy the light-heartedness of joking. Now you ought to hear Sam when he's instructing students on a subject, an idea they avoid because it's too deep, something they must think about to get a truthful meaning. The high school civics teacher invited his students to an assembly in the cabin to listen to Sam for over an hour. Sam started by reading from the notes he prepared, and then he just let it flow. Meredith pushed me to go, and I'm glad I did because that was another attraction, ah, that magnetic string that drew me to him."

It goes quiet around the table as they concentrate on the pizza. Mark finishes chewing his last bite and then says, "So, what's the schedule for tomorrow? When do you leave for the office?"

"The office opens at eight. I'll knock on your door at six."

"Six?" Susan questions.

"Sure, why not? You can fix me some of your pancakes I love." Francinea replies.

Three

    Sam sits down at the desk the following day, looking out the frosty window reflecting on the last few days' events. He starts typing.

    My Cabin Life 18

    Oh, where do I start, as there's so much going on now? King getting skunked. Meeting Joyce in the laundromat. Mark and Susan at the diner. Our plans for Thanksgiving. Learning of Harry and Meredith.

    Oh, the wonders of it all. When King got skunked, I thought: why did this have to happen, especially now when we're planning on a big Thanksgiving event? It put more pressure on me. Would that smell be evident for weeks? Who would want to come when the cabin reeked like that? Yuck, I yelled out loud.

    And then, after dropping King to let the professionals handle that, I stopped at the only laundromat in town. The owner helped and offered suggestions on cleaning the truck and my cabin. Then at the diner, Joanna introduced me to visitors coming to surprise Francinea.

Wow. The workings of the behind-the-scenes magnificent almighty God, the wonders of our invisible creator working in the present background to help me, a mere mortal in the woods.

If King had not gotten sprayed, I wouldn't have met Joyce. I wouldn't have met those wonderful friends of Francinea. And, I wouldn't be here typing while waiting for their visit. No, King and I may have gone for a walk, and I'd be alone thinking of our plans for Thanksgiving.

Yes, Lord, thank You for directing King's curiosity to get close and disturb that skunk.

Okay, enough of that this morning. Francinea is bringing her friends over soon, so I must tidy up this place a bit. Make it warmer. Samuel adds three logs to the fireplace and two to the stove. He takes King's food bowl to the sink and wipes it fresh. He sets a pot of water on the stove to warm so he can clean the stash of several days' dirty dishes, pans, and silverware left in the big sink. He removes the dry clothes hanging on the line, folds them, and puts them in the closet and dresser, and then he neatly folds the quilt, places it at the foot of the bed, puffs the pillows, and straightens the blanket covering the sheets. In the bathroom, he cleans the mirror, the commode, slides the curtain to cover the tub, throws the used towels into the basket of dirty laundry, and puts clean ones on the rack. And then he pumps more water into the tank above the commode. He straightens the blankets and pillows on the couch and side chair facing the fireplace, and then at the desk, he removes a partially written memo, crumbles it, and throws it in the basket. He looks around the cabin. "The bookcase? No. Guess that'll do, then."

He then slides into the pair of boots, dons a sweatshirt, leather jacket, gloves, and is about to open the door when he sees the pot of water boiling. "Gads." Sam quickly grabs the two handles and moves the pot to the counter next to the sink, where he sees the dirty dishes he wanted to wash. He looks at his watch. "Later."

On the porch, he pauses to look over the area and walks to the gazebo area. He punches the cushions and turns them over to dry the damp bottoms in the sun. Satisfied, Samuel walks toward the stream to look at the waters flowing into the lake. He turns and starts the trek through the woods, following the stream to the highway. Reaching the road, Samuel turns and walks next to the tree line rather than along the roadside. A car passes, tooting its horn. Then, one slows, and the passenger hollers "Sam!" out the window while waving her arm. He waves back, recognizing her as Susan, Jimmy's wife.

Now at the road to his cabin domain, he pauses and thinks. *I could stay here and wait for Fran and her friends to arrive.* "Nope, go back inside where it's warmer."

Samuel is approaching the porch when he hears a vehicle tooting its horn. He turns to look, and there it is, Francinea's SUV coming around the bend. The car stops in front of his porch.

"Here we are, ready or not," Francinea announces as she opens her door.

"Ah, come here. Mark and Susan, now you can see the inside." Sam says, raising his voice, pointing his arm toward the garden, then the gazebo, the lake view, and the cabin and his barn.

Susan says, "Fran, like I told Sam yesterday, It's like a National Geographic photo I've seen. Beautiful. Oh, Fran. Are you sure it's Sam you love, or is it this atmosphere?"

"Both!" Francinea answers and then adds, "Come on, see the inside."

Samuel opens the door for Susan, Francinea, and then Mark, who asks, "How many acres?"

"Ten and a part." Samuel quickly answers. "It's from a stream to the east and the National Forest boundary on the west."

Susan takes in the kitchen area as Mark rubs his hand over the varnished inside logs and molding. He ponders the bookcase and moves to get a closer look at the fireplace as Samuel pulls Francinea in a hug, a quick touch of their lips.

After feeling the pieces of stone at the fireplace, Mark says, "I've heard stories of a family with a similar stone fireplace where the original owners assigned a particular stone to each member of the family."

Samuel replies, "interesting. Yeah, Fran, we could start that."

"Samuel," Susan says. " How often do you wash these dishes? Show me what to do."

"Ah, no. I'll get them later."

"Fran, do you know? Have you done it before? Come on, show me."

"It's quite a process, Francinea replies. "Come over here and see the bathroom, the closet, and the bed area. But first, take a look at this." She slides the curtain for Susan to see shelves full of canned items. "All of those jars were the work of Sam's grandmother."

"How long ago was that?"

"Each jar is dated."

Samuel then relates to Susan and Mark of his grandparents' self-reliance life of growing their food. Her cooking skills and classes she held for local people. His fishing and hunting, work with the boy scouts, and the stories he read to kids in the library. "He was born right there on a couch by the fireplace and lived here 94 years." Sam pauses, "And that's the overwhelming legacy I'm trying to live up to."

Francinea then says, "Sam is getting noted around town as following along in his grandfather's steps. But Sam, where's the stew you were going to prepare for us?"

"Well, I didn't find a skunk, and where are the sandwiches from the diner? Did you forget?"

"No, I skipped that as I wanted to get here early to disturb your napping."

"Oh yeah, then you might have heard my snoring." Samuel leans over toward Mark and Susan, now comfortable on the couch, "Would you like to go for a walk? Fran can stay here and wash those dishes." Sam gets a belly punch. He starts singing, "I knew you were coming, but I forgot to bake ... er, find a skunk."

Fran quickly looks at Susan and then replies, "he's gonna get a cake he'll never forget. Skunk oil topping." She breathes deeply, "ah, enough of that. Let's go for that walk." She grabs Sam's hand in hers and nods to Susan, "Come on. You'll love it."

"We took a short walk yesterday."

"We'll take a different path," Samuel replies. Samuel leads them first to the gazebo area for a good view of the lake's calm waters reflecting the forest rising to the snow-capped mountains.

"Like I said earlier," Susan states. "It's like a cover for National Geographic. Honey, get a picture of this. Fran, you and Sam stand right there." She points to a spot as Mark gets his cell phone ready.

"Smile!"

"See, that's another useful thing for cell phones." Susan declares.

Sam leads them to the path to the right of the pier and the restricted national forest area, up the slope a bit, and then backtrack along the shoreline to the path leading back to the gazebo. Mark has taken many pictures along the way and several views of the cabin. "Here, rest a bit," Sam suggests. They quietly sit and look over the lake and up to the mountaintops. "I've peacefully sat right here numerous times to let the mind wander, and I'd get wondered by it all."

"What'd you got in the barn?" Mark asks.

"Mostly tools, plowing equipment for the garden, and the wood for the fireplace. A few stalls and a sleigh. Gramps had a horse he used for tilling the garden and to pull the sleigh." Sam notices Susan pulling on her coat. "You look like you're getting chilly. Let's go warm up by the fireplace."

They walk back into the cabin, remove the coats and gloves, and sit on the couch, as Sam adds more cut wood to the diminishing flames and then leans back against the chair's cushion.

"Fran," Susan then says. "We've got one more day, as we got to head back Thursday, so what else do you want us to see."

Francinea answers, "You've met Meredith, but ah, not her boyfriend, Harry. They'll both be in school, and I must be at the office in the morning. Around town, nothing impressive. Sam, you could entertain them."

"Sure. Would you be up for a ride in the boat to get a view from the lake? Or, we could play a board game." Sam answers and then says, "Oh, in the morning, I've got to get my dog, but the rest of the day is open. Hey, how about this? We'll go to Johnsonville for dinner, and they'd see Harry at work."

"No, Sam, remember, he only works the weekends. Sue, I'll make a few calls in the morning. Maybe I'll be able to postpone some afternoon appointments. I'll let you know."

"Sam, you do need a phone for times like this," Mark says

"No juice to keep them charged." Samuel quickly replies.

"They've got battery-operated chargers now."

"Ah, no thanks. I can do without it."

"But Sam," Susan interjects. "You'd be able to keep in touch with Fran while she's working, or she may have to get in touch with you. A delay or change in plans, an accident, anything. Yes, you must get a phone."

Sam looks at Fran, who appears to like the idea. "Hmm? We'll talk about it. But, so far, I've learned and welcomed a life outside the technology grid. No TVs, radios, computers. None of that stuff. And, lately, I've been thinking of getting a horse for transportation instead of that pickup. All the old-timers like Lincoln, Washington, St. Paul, and Moses survived quite well without that. Yeah, ponder the distances Paul traveled without, well, no maps or a stop for a sandwich at McDonald's' and to use the restroom. I'm enjoying this freedom. I'm not scared or apprehensive at all." Sam pauses, looking back at Francinea. "Oh, I better shut up."

Susan, peering at Francinea, says, "Fran, are you sure you want to embrace this? It's a beautiful romantic setting. I hope that isn't all."

"Huh? Why you asking me that?" Francinea responds. "You think I haven't thought this through?"

"Oh, I'm just thinking of the possibilities. You're working, and Sam could get hurt again and need immediate help. Or, something could happen to you. He'd be wondering." Susan breathes deeply. "Mark is right. A cell phone, such a simple and reasonable, must have to communicate in times of need. That's all I'm saying."

"Well, ha, ha, ha," Francinea answers. "We haven't told you everything. Another part of this is that we will embrace it just like Adam and Eve did at first. Covered with leaves."

Recognizing Fran's look, Sam says, "Yeah. Sounds good. We'll require that for the Thanksgiving meeting."

"Fran, you're playing that game again." Susan declares. "But I'm not. I'm serious. The cell phone is a necessity. And please, seriously, reconsider this." She turns her head toward Sam. "I have nothing against you, Sam, but your denial to get a phone seems to be pretentious. Is it so you can state how independent you are? Sorry, but that's how I see it."

"Hey, no problem. If that's the way you see it, then, well, that's how you see it. Come on, let's go for another walk in the woods," Sam interjects to change the subject. He gets off the chair, takes Fran by the hand, and signals Mark and Susan, "Come on. It's a beautiful sunny day. Why waste it? Let's go down to the pier for a good relaxing lake-side view."

They rise from the couch, and Francinea interjects, "No, let's go eat. Sam, the diner, or that Home Town restaurant in Johnsonville?"

On the way to the car, Francinea leans into Samuel, whispering, "she's getting on my nerves. They both are."

During the ride to the restaurant, Mark and Susan quietly admire the landscape's curvature scenery with the background's white-capped mountains. Mark has his cell phone camera pointed at and recording the view. Suddenly, Samuel brakes and pulls to the left as a couple of doe's scamper across the road.

"Whew!" Samuel quirks as he steers the car back into his lane.

"Wow!" Susan mutters as she straightens from the unexpected.

Mark quickly says, "Oh, I wish I had the camera focused on that instead of the scenery off to the left."

"The deer don't read our signs," Sam remarks.

"Yes, that'd be a good one for your next article," Susan notes to Mark. Then she leans forward and touches Francinea's shoulder. "That's another usefulness of cell phones."

It's a quiet ride the next five minutes into Johnsonville.

"We shouldn't have a problem being seated at this time," Samuel says. "About four, the lines get longer, sometimes to around the block." The tall sign comes into view. Sam turns the corner, pulls into the lot, and parks the car in the second row next to the entrance. "Here we are. No waiting now."

Samuel and Francinea follow Mark and Susan when their names get called and then step through the trellis. The young man greets and leads them to a booth, hands each their personal menus, and introduces their waitress, Andrea, standing next to him.

"Enjoy your special meal, and thanks," The greeter says and leaves. Andrea sets down the covered glasses of water, straw and says, "Thank you. You each have three choices of the main dish and three sides to choose from. I'll give you a few minutes, but first, an update. Coffee is no longer available, but you can choose hot tea instead. Anyone?"

"No more coffee?" Sam exclaims.

"Yes, sir. India tea is better. Direct from the fertile fields, harvested especially for us."

"Yes, we'll have some," Susan announces.

"Tea for the Bannisters," Andrea checks the spot on the tablet.

"Try it, Mr. Guardyall. It's good and healthy too, more so than coffee." Andrea informs him.

"Hot chocolate for me," Francinea says.

"We don't serve that either," Andrea replies.

"Just the water, then," Francinea announces as she removes the plastic covering on the glass.

"Okay, I'll go for the tea," Samuel says. "Black. No sugar." Andrea enters their choices into the tablet and leaves.

Susan and Mark briefly look the menu over. Susan relates that a similar restaurant opened in Indianapolis a few months ago, and it's become the place to go.

"I tried this when I first arrived and haven't been back since," Samuel says. "To me, it's a brief look at more and more of how the feds enter our private lives."

Susan responds, "Oh, come on, Sam. It's good to know that they do care for us and want to help us maintain healthy standards. The hospitals aid patients by providing food that they individually need, not desire. And, Sam, you need a cell phone."

"Sue, we've been friends for a long time," Francinea interjects. "And we've always wanted the best for each other. Don't you want us to be happy in our way? What's going on? Why the change?"

"No, no, no, I do want you to be happy. I'm simply inferring that if I were in your shoes, I'd insist on the cell phone. That simple tool will be a blessing sometime, and you'll be glad you did. It could be the difference between life or death, or whatever. Sam, you must reconsider this. Do it for Fran's sake."

Samuel answers. "A year ago, I had it all; computers, the newest smartphones, my drafting software, and of course, the TV mesmerizing entertainment. Yes, I used it all to advance my business. But moving here and embracing this lifestyle, I vowed that I would go without it. And, the feds will not allow me to connect to the power grid. Please, try to understand this change I've willingly accepted." He sighs while softly thumping his fingers. "That's all I got to say, so please no more."

Francinea reaches under the table to squeeze Sam's hand.

Sam adds, "Let's put that aside for now and enjoy our time together. It's great that you took the time to travel this far for Fran."

Mark breaks in the discussion, "We're going to take the southern route, through Oklahoma and Arkansas. But it will take another half-day or more. We'll then see more of the Arkansas hills."

Francinea tried hard not to get upset by Susan's further statements about the changed lifestyle's seriousness during dinner, such as, "Sam, you could move in with Fran and use the cabin as, well, a retreat, a weekend campfire."

Sam ignores her and questions Mark and his work.

"I've been coaching a high school baseball team for eighteen years and write a column about current local and state events for the Weekly Times. That takes a lot of time to keep up-to-date on what's happening locally and around the state."

Several times, Samuel referred to the blessings of being free spiritually and physically well knowing that whatever happens, there's a reason why. "Because my dog got sprayed, I had time to stop at the diner, and we met before you surprised Fran. And, if I had not cut my leg, I would not have met Francinea."

On the way back to the cabin, Mark and Susan quietly talk in the back seat and then announce that they felt they had to leave in the morning instead of staying another day. The weather forecast was not good is the excuse they used.

Samuel slowly maneuvers Francinea's SUV down his road to the cabin and stops in front of the porch, "Well, here I am." He opens the car door, looks up, and stares at the full moon. He leans over to tell them, "Oh, take a look at this."

The three of them open the doors and look up when Sam tells them. "At home, I never had such a view as the street lights, and traffic hindered the brilliant view of a full moon along with those thousands of stars providing nighttime navigation."

"Yes, it is, " Mark says. "You've got a beautiful place here, Sam. We hope the best for you and Fran."

"Thanks," Samuel says. "I pray to God that your trip will be pleasant, and you'll arrive safely. You two take care and remember our Lord God is beside you along the way."

"Sorry, Sam," Susan tells him. "But we must go." They shake hands and get back into the car.

Francinea hugs and kisses Sam before she gets in the driver's seat. "I'll stop by tomorrow evening. Bye, honey." She closes the door and drives off.

Four

Wednesday morning comes to Sam without a lick from King. He finishes his morning routine. He fires up the fireplace and stove, fixes his coffee, eats the banana on the porch, and then his juice by the fireplace. He relaxes on the couch as he reads his morning devotions plus the journey of reading the Bible thru in one year. Finishing that, he carries his coffee to the desk and starts writing his thoughts about near-future plans.

Ah, where do I start? So much is happening.

"Wait, I wrote all this down the other day." He pulls the sheet out, crumbles it, and dumps it in the basket. *Why did I forget that? What's happening? Early sign of dementia?* "No, this cannot be," he lifts his voice. "I am like a free-flying eagle, so get lost, you demon."

Now it's time for a good morning walk in the woods. He slides into those boots, dons a sweatshirt, the jacket, cap, and gloves, opens the door, steps on the porch, and glances over the treetops. He strolls toward the lake's rippled waters and continues to the western boundary and up the tree-lined path to the road. Crossing it, Sam walks alongside the ditch a few minutes and stops at an older path leading into the southern forest. Looking to his left and right, and another peek up the over-grown weedy way deep into the woods, he ponders, "Yeah, why not?" Twenty minutes or so into the forest, he comes upon an opening. "Wow! Beautiful." *I've been here for six months, and no one told me about this?*

There's a wooden bench off to his right, then another one and another, each spaced ten yards apart. He sits, raises his arms to rest on the back, and peers over the scene of a medium-sized lake, a waterfall on the left dumping gallons and gallons of water into a stream pouring into the lake.

"Oh, if my cabin were situated here, I'd be sitting here for hours."

About a half-mile across the lake are four pillars of copper-toned ridges pointing to the heavens. *If I had my binoculars, I could get a closer look at what could be two guys who seem to be climbing upwards on the tallest of the peaks.* He leans back and looks heavenward at the puffy white clouds slowly mingling with others. To his right, a stream separates the forest, slowly rising on both sides. He gets up and starts to walk past the benches and into the woods again, carefully stepping on the fallen leaves and twigs and periodically looking back, wondering where the path will lead him to next. *My legs are getting tired.* But he keeps going. A few minutes later, he sees a sign in the distance.

Approaching it, he reads,

STOP.

NO ONE IS ALLOWED BEYOND THIS POINT.
TURN AROUND AND GO BACK.
THIS IS FEDERALLY PROTECTED PROPERTY.

DO NOT PROCEED

"Hmm? Feds protecting it? No one here." He takes a few steps around the sign, and a section of barbed wires rises off the path to waist-high. About twenty yards ahead, he sees a wolf, big left eye, ready to jump. He takes a concentrated look, "that's fake." He turns and heads back to the benches to rest his legs. Looking again at the peaks, he peers at the spot where he thought two guys were climbing. "Nothing there now," he mumbles. *What's going on with me today? My eyes?* He closes his eyes and blinks a few times. He rubs under each eye, blinks again, and looks out. "Oh well." He stands and starts the trek along the path back to the road and to the cabin, gets the keys to the truck, and drives into town. He finds a parking spot and enters the diner.

"Well, Samuel, good morning." Joanna greets him and points him to a small table in the restaurant's narrow rear area. On the way, he sees George and his wife.

"Good morning, George and Ethel. No millwork this morning?" Samuel asks.

"Yep. We have the day off as our saws need overhauls."

"I'll get back to you soon about a proposal, possibly Thanksgiving evening. Still working on the details." Samuel tells them.

"Oh Sam, we'll be out of town that week," Ethel says.

"Hmm? Then I guess it'll wait. Get in touch when you get back." He turns as Joanna approaches with his cup of coffee, nudging him to grab a seat at another table.

"Thanks," Samuel tells Joanna. "Just two of your blueberry pancakes. Busy morning?"

"Got it. Yes, it has been," she says as her jaw enjoys the gum.

"Hey, Joanna. You've been here for a long time. What do you know about the Federally protected area off the road to the southwest?"

"Ah, you've been out exploring again. Didn't you see the sign on the path?"

"No. There was no sign there."

"Hmm," Joanna answers and then sits on the chair opposite him when she quietly asks. "Did you come upon some benches?"

"Yes, and past that the big sign."

"Ah, it's supposedly some sort of training area—top-secret. No one is supposed to know anything more. I'm surprised you were able to get that far."

"Nobody around anywhere except for two guys climbing the pillars across the lake."

"Sam, I can't say anything more, and I'll erase this from my memory." She rises, "I'll be back with the pancakes. And, Sam, don't ask anyone about that area, especially the sheriff? You'll put him in a difficult spot."

Samuel finishes his pancakes, takes the last sip of coffee, pays Joanna at the check-out, and heads to the Vet to get his dog.

King paws over Samuel on the drive back to the cabin. "Now, King, don't do that again."

"Woof, woof." King barks in Sam's face. "Oh, you thought it was fun, huh? Was it fun to be caged for three days?"

As the truck nears the barn, King starts barking like crazy, paws down on the handle, and the door opens. He jumps out, running around the familiar territory.

Inside the cabin, Sam refreshes the fireplace and the stove, makes more coffee, and sits on the couch to read a book while the dog does his thing around the area. About an hour later, Sam lets King inside and adds more wood to the fireplace. *Oh, I should have asked George to bring more wood out this week. What's going on? My memory seems to be slipping. Any other time, I would have reminded him about the wood supply.* Sam goes back to the book by Francis Schaeffer.

At lunchtime, Sam starts to prepare a fish dinner for Francinea. Standing over the sink, pumping water over the two-rainbow trout, King straightens up, barks, and trots toward the door. Looking out the window, Sam sees the familiar truck backing up to the barn.

"It's George with the wood. Yippee." Sam sets the trout on a plate next to the sink, slides into warm outerwear, and then goes out to greet him. King gets there first pawing on George.

"Hey, buddy," George says as he runs his hand over the dog's neck and shoulders. "Howdy Sam. How's everything?"

"Better now, as the stack was low and hoped you didn't forget. Steven, how's dad treating you today?"

"Ah, the usual," Steven replies as he positions the roller tracks from the truck's tailgate to the bench inside the barn. Slowly Sam and George place the bundles of six next to the diminished stack. About twenty bundles get stacked in the stall, and Sam suggests: "Hey George, let's put the rest up there on the porch."

"Sure." Steven moves the truck in front of the porch steps, and they start unloading each bundle next to the door and wall.

"Sam," George asks. "Have you ever ventured off the road and south into the woods? Surely, knowing your curiosity, you have, right?"

"Huh? Why do you ask?"

"After you left the diner, an FBI agent I've known approached and asked me about you. They have snapshots of you sitting on the bench and then going further in."

"Hmm?" Samuel softly replies. "Yes, I did earlier this morning." *Now he asked me. How could I refuse to say anything after George brought it up?* "While at the diner, I asked Joanna about that area, and she said it was some sort of a training post, but I shouldn't say anything more about it to anyone, even the sheriff.

So, what's going on there that's so secret, and why did he ask you about me?"

"Sam," George says. "You know, I've lived my entire life right here in Prairieville. That area you entered this morning was declared a national forest the same time as the land surrounding this cabin. The thousand acres we get our wood from are surrounded by the federal property, and we've been butting heads with them ever since, as they want our land too. They claim one of our mill workers committed suicide by hanging himself from a tree behind those benches. And since then, we've all been monitored closely. If they show up here, be careful with what you ask and respond to their questioning."

"Joanna also asked about a sign somewhere. There was no sign anywhere along the path I walked. Just the one further away from the benches."

"Be careful, Sam," George exclaims. He takes a deep breath and says, "We've got to go. I've got you scheduled for another load in a couple of weeks. We've got more to do. See ya."

And off they go, leaving Sam wondering. He pours himself a fresh cup of coffee and leans back in the rocker. "Okay, Lord, lead me this afternoon if they show up." He opens the book to the bookmarked page of 'Escape From Reason.'

He reads a paragraph or two, then starts to re-read it. "Quiet down, mind." Having trouble concentrating on the book, Sam pushes the thoughts of the possible meeting aside, and starts reading again, desiring to finish the book by Francis Shaeffer.

Mid-afternoon, King runs to chase a black vehicle entering the open area and stops next to the truck.

"King!" Sam yells at his dog, now with his paws on the door. "Come here! SIT!"

Two men in black uniforms get out and approach Samuel on the porch.

The one driving the vehicle says, "afternoon. You're Samuel Guardyall? Am I right?"

"Yes, I'm Samuel. And you are?"

"Michael Fontenal, and this is Jeffery Boonactir."

"So, what can I do for you today," Samuel asks, noticing the small FBI insignia on their shoulders. "Hey, I've got coffee warming inside. Come on in out of the cold." Samuel turns and opens the Dutch door leading the guys into his cabin. He tells King, "Stay!"

"Cream, sugar?" Samuel asks as he gets two cups off the shelf.

"Black is fine, and thanks."

Sam puts two cups on the table. He sips his cup and remains standing, noticing that Jeffery is meandering around the cabin, looking at everything, the rafters, the bookcase, the bed area, the fireplace, the desk, and the typewriter. He slides open the curtain to look inside the closet.

Michael sips his coffee and says, "So, over the past six months, how are you adjusting to this rural antique lifestyle? It's a nicely accommodated cabin. We've learned that you intend to keep this property just as it was. Is that right?"

"Yes, I've made that determination," Sam replies. "Michael, if I may, I'd like to confess a transgression I unknowingly did this morning. It seems that I trespassed into the federal off-limits area south of the road. I was out for a stroll this morning when I ventured upon a path into those woods. I came upon the benches and was captivated by the beautiful area. I must have sat there for perhaps ten, fifteen minutes and then strolled further into the forest to that sign and the pop-up wired gate. That was it. I turned around and walked back to the road and returned here. I suppose you're here to reprimand me."

As Jeffery sits at the table, his right hand reaches under the table as his left lifts the cup to his lips.

Sam puts his hands together on the table in front of Michael. "Are you going to arrest me for trespassing?"

Michael takes a glance at Jeffery and then says, "Ah." He pauses, takes a breath, and continues, "No, there's no need to do that. Samuel, we came here to get acquainted and let you know that land is a protected area. New signs and gates will be set in place soon. The fish and wildlife folks have indicated that you've not violated intrusion into the forest surrounding your acreage on the east and west side, which is also part of the Federal forest."

"Yes, I've been close but haven't gone into it… yet. Can I ask a question? Why don't you come sometime for a visit, a fireplace chat, and hear my testimony of how much God loves each of us. This God of all sent his only son, an integral part of himself, as a sacrifice and redemption of our human waywardness. Boy, oh boy, I needed that. Yes, please. Please consider that. I'd enjoy the company as I sometimes feel the loneliness of this antique lifestyle."

"Thank you, Samuel. But you know that our position does not allow us to socialize with those we investigated. You are now aware of the restrictions on entering that territory. We've done our job, so we must go."

"But really, what's going on in there that is so secret to us citizens?"

"Mr. Guardyall, I can't say any more. Your job is to respect our property, and that's it."

"Well, okay. You guys respect mine too, so I'll abide by your rules."

"Good day then. I will submit a report of this, and they'll send you and the sheriff a copy in the mail. You now know we're watching out for you, for your safety and well-being here in your protected area. Thank you."

They get back into the black vehicle and leave Sam watching as King, barking like crazy, follows them out.

Five

    Sam wakes up Friday morning with a mild headache. He lets King out, peels, and eats a banana while waiting for the coffee water to warm in the pot on the stove. He reignites the charred wood in the fireplace, then looks at a partially written note on the typewriter and at his watch. *"Hmm? 8:15. Wonder how and when Mark and Susan got on the road this morning. Yes, Fran and I need to talk about that dang cell phone idea. Will she stop by here this evening? We need to discuss our plans for Thanksgiving.*

    He gulps some coffee as he looks out the window over the sink and sees King barking alongside the sheriff's car coming into view.

    "Well, good morning, Sheriff." Sam greets him as he steps onto the porch. "Come on in, and good to see you."

    "Good morning, Sam. Hmm! Looks like you just got up."

    "Yeah, slept in. Nothing important this morning, so I turned over for more. Here, have a cup." He cleans a dirty cup in the sink, dries it, fills it, and hands it to the sheriff. "Oh, oh," Sam mumbles, noticing the look on the sheriff's face. "What did I do now?"

"Thanks," the sheriff says, taking the cup from Sam. He sits down on one of the high chairs at the butcher block table and takes a quick sip. "Sam, I thought I told you about the area south of the road that you must not go into that part of the forest."

"If you did, I didn't recall any warning that it was off-limits federal property. Yes, I was out for a walk, and well, I guess you've heard about my curiosity. Two FBI guys came and confronted me about it. On another note, is there a cell phone that just makes and receives calls? None of the web stuff, weather and email, just calls."

"Well, yes. There is. I think they're called dumb phones with just talk and text communication." He takes a deep breath, sips the coffee. "Sam, you've got to restrain your adventurous wanderings."

"Why?" Sam asks. "What is going on in there that is so secretive? I thought I even saw what looked like a golden dome and possibly a runway out beyond those pillars. Come on, tell me more."

"Sam, all I can say is don't go in there again. Never! And don't mention it to anyone else."

"What's so secretive about it? Something is going on in there. As a citizen, don't we have the right to know?"

"All I can say is what I know. Years ago, the feds reprimanded your grandfather for his wanderings. He was in there watching them build those pillars, and an officer ordered that he leave and never come back. That's when they put the signs up. They wanted him arrested for trespassing, but the sheriff back then refused. A week or so later, the sheriff went missing, and after a month, a local found his body in a ditch outside Johnsonville. Supposedly he committed suicide, is what the coroner stated."

"Oh, wow! Okay, sheriff, I'm getting the message."

"Thanks." He puts the coffee to his lips, sets the cup down, rises off the stool. "There's a storm heading this way. Looks like a big one. The forecast is for a foot or more. Do you have enough wood to keep warm?" The sheriff asks, taking the few steps to the door, followed by Sam.

"Yes, George brought me a bunch the other day. Am I allowed to keep a secret from the feds? You're a friend so let me tell you MY secret." Sam pauses, breathes deeply, and sighs. "Francinea said yes to my proposal. We plan on announcing it on Thanksgiving and have the ceremony here in June."

"Wow! Congratulations."

"And, she's agreed to living here. She'll continue working her practice, spend the evenings and weekends here. We want you and Mary to come to the announcement party."

"King will get jealous," the sheriff grins. "You may have to get him a mate."

Sam chuckles at the remark.

"Well, Sam, I've got to go. Remember that the area south of the road to Johnsonville is off-limits, and don't . . . ah, please, for me and you, don't bring this subject up again. Okay." The sheriff pauses, thinking. "Ah, oh yeah. Did you see anything at all in your grandfathers' notes about that event I mentioned about the sheriff back then? He may have written something about it."

Sam, rubbing his forehead, thinks back. "Not that I recall right now. They dated that journal, so what year was it?"

"Somewhere in the '60s, I believe."

"Wow! He would've been in his 30's, and his father was still living then. So perhaps it was my great grandfather who experienced that."

"Could be."

"Now, sheriff, this is intriguing, and I will search this out deeper in his notes to see what I can find. If I do discover more, would you like to know? And, just the two of us."

"Yes, I would. Give me a call. Sam, here's my personal phone number, so when you get that phone, use it to call me rather than buzzing the office." The sheriff gets off the chair, and on the way to the door, he says, "Sam, I trust you, and that's why I came to let you know what's going on. Okay, so no more."

"Thanks a bunch. God is watching over you, and that retirement will soon be yours to enjoy." They shake hands. He leaves as King follows the van up the drive and out of sight. And then, the dog runs back to Samuel, relaxing on the rocking chair. He reaches down and rubs his ears and neck. "Hey, would you like a mate, one just like you that you can explore the area with?" King barks a few times and then settles down next to the rocker, his tongue moving in and out.

Samuel pets his dog and then goes inside the cabin. He refreshes his coffee and goes over to the bookcase. On the bottom shelf, he chooses a hard-back brown cover. He opens it and then puts it back on the shelf. *"That was part of grandma's recipes. Now, if he did write a journal, where would granddad have put it? I didn't see anything like that in the foot-locker."* Samuel then goes to the closet and searches the shelves and cases. He starts pulling the labeled shoeboxes off the top shelf on his right and looks inside each. He finds nothing resembling a journal or notebook. *"Humm! Surely, if granddad had experienced anything like what the sheriff had indicated, he would have written something about it. I would have."* He slides the curtain back, goes over to the desk, and puts a blank paper in the typewriter. He starts pushing the keys.

My Cabin Life 19

Here I am again with a puzzle. What is going on in that federal land off the road on the left? I've been admonished to never again bring that up in any conversation, even with the sheriff. How about Francinea? Can I tell her of my meanderings? She'll be my wife, and we can't have any secrets. Did grandpa and his father write about it? Grandpa was in his thirties at the time. He would have known about the threats, and perhaps he was the one who was threatened, or was it his dad? Did either of them jot it down somewhere? I certainly would have made notes about that. Did they write about it? Okay, on to another subject, that of a cellphone. Yes? No? The sheriff said there's one that is strictly a phone, naming it a dumb phone. No web stuff at all. I'm leaning in that direction, as I can see its usefulness as it allows calls only. Back in the old days, those original wired telephones were a tremendous blessing to folks all over the country. Then came the television, the computers, and now, a handheld device does all that a computer, a telephone, and tv do. Whatever?

Well, Lord, what's next for me?
And, where is that somewhere?

He leaves the note in there to possibly add more to that remembrance later. "Ready, King? Let's go for a walk."

"Woof, woof, woof," his pet remarks and beats Sam to the door. Samuel dons his jacket, the Cubs hat Mark had given him, gloves, and he slides into his boots. He looks up at the clear blue sky and then to the northwest; he sees deep gray clouds not too far away. "Ah, King, a storm is heading our way. so this will be a short one."

He, with King following close alongside, pass the boat dock and into the western woods. King dashes off ahead of Sam. "Wait! Stop! King, COME!" Soon the dog is back alongside Sam, wanting rubs. They turn and tread to the dock, where Sam reaches for the rope tying the rowboat. He pulls the boat up onto the shore and turns it over. King runs to Sam with a tennis ball, and Sam tries to grab it. But King, backing up, holds it tight. "You want to go fetch, but you won't let go. How can I throw it?" The dog drops the ball, barks, and picks it up again. "Okay, have it your way," Sam says, and picks up a rock and throws it up to the Gazebo area. With the tennis ball still in his jaws, King takes off after the rock.

Samuel watches King while walking to the barn. He takes the extra set of keys off the hook, starts the pick-up, and drives it into the barn. He then checks on the snowplow, the wide shovel, and brooms. "Now it's time to rest a bit. Come on, buddy, we'll go warm up." King sits with the tennis ball locked in his jaws, then drops it at Sam's feet. "More playtime, eh! Okay, one more." Sam throws it as far as he can toward the pier, and King takes off.

Sam re-fills his coffee and sits down at the typewriter. He reads the last Cabin Life memo he typed. He starts typing again when a thought breezes across his mind. *"Yes, that's where it is. I saw that but never got into it."* Sam hurries to the bed area, opens the footlocker, and neatly sets the scrapbooks of pictures aside. His hands now carefully lift a tan hardback book, opens it, and sees a hand-written note.

Notes by Marie Anton Guardyall
Daughter to Marjorie and Joseph T. VonKamp.
Born February 2, 1904
  Johnsonville Colorado.

"Wow!" Samuel exclaims. "That's my great-grandmother." He carefully turns the tarnished page noting the date on top and then reads an entry.

Here I am on June 1, 1923, now the wife of Samuel Franklin. Guardyall. His first wife, June Wanton, passed away six months ago from Typhoid Fever. I then submitted and became his new wife right here in this cabin.. I love it.

July 22, 1924.

What a joy it has been to bring a child into this world. Together, we named him Joshua Abram Guardyall.

"My grandfather," Samuel mutters. He turns a few pages.

August 22, 1936

Samuel and Joshua stopped collecting the corn during the rain and hail storm. The winds the roof the barn off.

August 29, 1936

With the help of friends, the roof is finished. We held a feast for all.

"Oh, boy!" *What a treasure this is. But will there be a note in here about that event the sheriff mentioned?"* He carefully turns page after page looking for more current dates. Three-quarters of the way through, he sees the year 1960 and a note by his grandmother Amilia.

May 10, 1960

Joshua had to put down one of the horses this morning. Sheriff Brownstein came to help. He and June stayed for dinner.

Samuel continues to scan the notes. "Here it is."

September 21, 1962. Friday
Oh, we're in trouble with the government. Joshua was caught trespassing in the newly declared national forest south of the gravel road to Johnsonville.

September 22
Our friend, the sheriff, resisted and would not arrest Joshua. All Joshua did was watch them build something. There were no signs saying keep out.

September 24 Early Monday morning.
We were visited by the government today.

September 25
The deputy came by today asking about the sheriff. He is unable to contact him. The town people are searching the woods. Boats are on the lake searching.

Everybody is concerned. June, and their three boys are being comforted by pastor Brunno, and the members are providing food.

September 27

The two government agents visited us again to remind us it's a new land treaty initiated by the war powers and was okayed by the Governor for our protection.

September 28

The city and county have argued with the government about restricting them from searching the forest for the sheriff. The mayor called the governor.

September 29

A rainstorm stopped the search. Now asking for help from the Mayor and Governor.

Sunday, September 30

Pastor Brunno held an outdoor service for the entire town to come and pray for the sheriff and his family.

October 1

The search continues further west beyond Johnsonville. The governor has sent his national guard men to help. Helicopters are circling the area. The government is now allowing people to search the national forest. Joshua, Franklin, Samuel Sr. and more are riding horses through those woods looking for the sheriff. The diner is bringing food. Joshua said the construction in that land had been put on hold.

October 2

The searching continues. The pastor holds a prayer breakfast.

October 4

People are ready to give up. June and the boys left town today.

October 5

The prayer breakfast continues. The national guard boys are walking through the ditches next to every road. They have dogs smelling.

Monday, October 8

The end. A dog discovered the half-buried decayed body of the sheriff in a ditch outside Johnsonville at

10:23 this morning. Later, the state coroner stated the sheriff had died from an overdose. Said he was drunk

Wednesday, October 10
The town gathers together in memory of Sheriff Brownstein.

"Oh," Samuel mutters out loud. "If I could only copy this for the sheriff, but it's too fragile." *I want Fran to see these notes and see what she thinks. Is she aware of the federal area? Would all this hamper her desire to move in with me feeling like I am, that they could do whatever to this property?* "Lord, help us and keep us aware and protected."

Samuel continues reading notes left by his grandmother Amilia and skips over others. One specifically caught his attention. It told of their joy when his father, Franklin informed them of his coming marriage to his mother and how wonderful the ceremony was right there at the gazebo. Samuel turns several more pages, and one grabs his attention. It relates the disagreements and almost a physical fight when his dad said he was leaving and never coming back.

November 26, 1979
As Franklin was leaving, Joshua told him he would be welcomed back as a prodigal son when he changed his ways. Otherwise, we don't want to see him again.

Finally, he turns to the last page in the journal, a note written by Joshua.

June 2015
Amilia has passed on to glory, and soon I will be joining her, but there is still work I must do. When my time comes to join the herd, I will leave all this to my grandson Samuel Jr. For his knowledge, I leave our heritage as far as known.

Samuel continues reading the names, birth and death dates, children's names, and spouses. *Wow, This goes back to the early 1800s when the first Guardyall immigrated here from Finland. My great-great-grandfather built this cabin in 1902.* Scanning his family lineage, their names, and their children down through the ages, he notes that the daughter of his great-great-great-grandfather: John Baptiste, married a lady named Marie Austra who had two boys and three girls. The first girl married a guy by the name of Ted R. Olsen.

"Could it be?"

Ethan Renew Guardyall 1847-1922
Purchased the land

John Baptiste Guardyall 1874-1946 Built this cabin with Ethan.

Samuel Nathan Guardyall 1898-1985
Added the closets and rest room

Joshua Abram Guardyall 1924-   (You Can fill in this date)

Franklin Dunkirk Guardyall 1949-1973
Your father

And now you.
Samuel Franklin Guardyall Junior 1968-

He closes the book and puts it back in the footlocker along with the scrapbooks, and pulls the cover down. He leans back against the bed, sighs, and mutters, "Thank You, Lord." He tilts his head against the bed and closes his eyes to rest a bit.

Six

Upon entering the cabin, Francinea sees Sam slouched beside the bed. "Sam, wake up! Are you all right?" She loudly says, kneeling beside him at the foot of the bed and rubbing his left shoulder and down his arm, wondering if he had a heart attack.

"Huh?" Sam says, opening his eyes and seeing Fran next to him. "Oh, I must have fallen asleep. King, back off!"

"Seeing you here like that, I got worried. What ya been doing?"

"Yes, I'm okay. More than okay, now that you're here.! Oh, the Lord directed me to a journal my grandmothers had written. It was in the bottom of this footlocker and out of sight. Oh, Fran, what a treasure. It provides many details of their lives."

"Someday, I'll want to read that, but right now, we've got to talk. I brought you a cup of coffee and a sandwich. Get up and join me on the couch." She grabs his forearm and helps him rise. They comfortably settle in on the couch. She hands him the coffee and the sandwich.

"What's on your mind?" he asks, taking a sip of coffee.

"Susan called yesterday and said they had an accident in Arkansas. The car is a total wreck, but they're fine, just some scrapes and bruises."

"Oh, no! Where in Arkansas?" Sam replies.

"Somewhere on the interstate. They were transported to a hospital, checked out, and are now in a motel. She just wanted to let me know. But, Sam, I'm worried about them. She was driving while Mark took a nap. She said a semi caused her to crash into the cement blocks dividing the lanes, and then the car bounced into a ditch."

"Thank God for keeping them safe."

"I think she wants me to get there somehow and drive them home, and I'm thinking about it."

Sam holds his hands out for Fran. "We'll pray and ask God to lead us, and them too." Slowly, he prays for guidance. "We'll wait till the morning and see if she calls again, or perhaps you would prefer to call her and get an update. Until then, let's wait, relax, and let God work. Now, let me show you the journal."

"Later, Sam," Fran softly remarks as she slides over next to him. He pulls her in close to lean her head against his shoulder. She takes a long deep breath and slowly sighs while closing her eyes.

He waits a bit and then asks, "Honey, what have you heard about the federal land south of the road?"

She does not respond. He nudges her. "Fran."

Nothing. No response. Sam lowers his head to view her face and eyes. He then pulls her in tighter to wake her but not startle her, and she raises her head from the restful position against him.

"You had a tough shift, didn't you?" Sam softly says.

"Huh? I dozed off?"

"Yes, you did."

"I'm sorry. You asked me something."

"Well, not important now. Let's grab a bite to eat at the diner."

"Okay, but your sandwich?"

"It'll wait." King follows them onto the porch, stops, and looks up at Sam. "Stay!" He instructs the dog.

"We'll take my car." Fran declares.

On the way to town, Fran relates some details of her day at the hospital. "This nurse I've known for some time refused to help. "My shift is over." She declared. "You'll have to get another nurse."

"Isn't that a kick in the face of that oath they take?"

"Yes, it is."

"Did you report it?"

"No. I'll talk with her Monday."

"And also," Fran adds. "Two small kids were kicked out of a car at the emergency door. They had been beaten with whips across their backs and fingers. We know nothing about who they are or belong to. I volunteered to help find the parents in the morning."

"Hospitals have surveillance cameras. Did they look at those pictures?"

"Yes, but can't tell if it was a man or a lady. The car was a white Camaro type. That's it."

"Well, that's a start. Anything else?"

"I don't know. I'll find out more in the morning."

"Tomorrow is Saturday. I thought we'd spend the day going over the details for Thanksgiving. Less than a week away. And, I'll have a big surprise for you."

"A few morning hours, that's all. We've got plenty of time for that. A surprise?"

"Yep, a big one too. Hey, you got a phone. I need to tell the sheriff about what I found." Sam reaches into his pocket for the sheriffs' private number. "Call this number."

Fran touches the numbers on her screen and holds the phone near Sam.

"Hello."

"Hey sheriff, this is Sam. I'm using Fran's phone. I found a journal you'd be interested in reading. And guess what? We're cousins."

"What? No way."

"Yes, like 3rd generation. You have a grandfather named Ted Olsen born in the early 1900s. He married the daughter of one of my great-great-grandparents, John Baptiste, born in 1879. Come on over sometime and look at the journal. It's all in there."

"Yes, Sam, I will. Sometime Sunday afternoon?" The sheriff pauses. "Francinea, are you there?"

"Yes, sheriff, I can hear you."

"Well, good. Sam informed me of your engagement. Congratulations! Knowing Sam as I do, you will have a great time together. Now, Fran, you've got my number on your phone, so if Sam does not treat you like a queen, call me, and I'll take care of him with my badge."

"Queen?" Sam quickly responds. "Then, that makes me the King. Hey, my queen, is breakfast ready?"

Fran punches Sam in the belly. Then tells the sheriff. "He's done it again. You might have to bring two deputies. Sam, my dear, in chess, Kings are limited to one space at a time, and Queens got freedom."

The sheriff interrupts. "You got my number, Fran. See you Sunday afternoon. Sam. Have that journal ready for me."

Fran hears the click and puts the phone in her purse. He's about to open the door.

"Wait, Sam, do you realize what you did?" Fran says, leaning over to get a good view of his expression.

"No! What did I do?"

"You violated one of your oaths, that rule of staying free of technology? You used my phone to tell the sheriff something."

"Oh my, I did, didn't I?" Sam repents. "Thanks. Tempted again, and without a thought, I gave in. Why? Yes, that's the nature of it, the easiness, the usefulness that draws us to accept and take part in all this technology. Thanks, Fran, you are my queen. Before deciding to embrace this lifestyle, I did some research about the Amish. They have managed to shun all technology and have remained separated from the secular world. I thought, if they can do it, I can do it. But they do use telephones for emergencies, but not cell phones. Yes, thanks again for pointing out my transgression against my own rules."

Sam parks the car near the diner. They're about to open the car door when through the windshield, they recognize George, Ethel, Jimmy, and Susan, exiting the diner. "Hey guys," Sam greets them. "We're about to go in, and you're leaving. How's Joanna today?"

"Susan and Ethel," Fran addresses the ladies approaching her side of the car. "There's something I need to discuss with you. Perhaps after church."

Susan, whispering, says, "There's a rumor going around about you and Sam. Is it true?"

"Rumor?" Fran questioned. "Which one? When Sam took me fishing, and I caught the biggest trout."

"Yeah, that's the one, and then he proposed to you right there in the boat." Ethel answers. "Congratulations! When's the big date?" Fran tries to dismiss the remark but can't hide her joy. She hugs the ladies squealing their glee, which gets the guys' attention chatting on the other side of the car.

"What's happening with them?" Jimmy asks, seeing the three ladies jumping up and down.

"Hmmm?" Samuel muses, "I think I know," He tells Jimmy and George as they walk around the front of the car.

"Honey," Ethel says to George. "Fran and Sam are engaged to be married. She wanted to keep it a secret until Thanksgiving, but our rumor mill works faster."

Fran grabs Sam's arm, and quietly tells him, "I couldn't help myself. It just came out."

After hearing the news, George and Jimmy rush to congratulate and shake Sam's hand, and Susan and Ethel take turns to hug him.

"So," Susan asks Fran after the celebration. "When and where?"

Fran hesitates a moment. "We haven't decided on any of that yet. Meredith is also engaged, and we were thinking of a mother-daughter wedding. That's it so far."

"Are you waiting for warmer weather in spring or summer?" Ethel says.

"Yes, why wait," Susan interjects. "New Year's Day falls on a Sunday this year. Do it then in the church. Get it over with. It's not like this is yours or Sam's first. Go for it quicker. I would."

Sam wraps his arm around Fran's waist, "yes, honey. Quick, like um, tomorrow."

"Sorry, but I've got to get back to work," George says. "Working today to fill in for that day off. See ya guys later, and good luck." He and Ethel drive off.

"Sam and Fran, we wish the best for you two," Jimmy says.

"We'll see you in church," Susan says.

"Honey, let's eat somewhere else. I saw Joanna looking at us out the window. Yes, I have two trout ready, and we could quietly talk this over in the cabin."

"Okay, but first, let's go to the animal clinic, and I can update Meredith. I'd rather she hear it from me than someone else."

They get back into the car. Looking to safely back up, he notices Joanna staring at him through the window. "Well, the rumor mill will be active," he states to Fran.

Arriving at the Vet's office, they walk hand in hand into the office. At the window, the clerk welcomes them and tells Francinea, "Meredith is assisting in an operation. She should be free in ten to fifteen minutes. Can I get you a drink or something?"

"Nah, we'll wait," Fran answers.

They sit and relax in the comfortable waiting room chairs. They each pick a magazine to page through and periodically show the other a picture or article about pets and how they instinctively behave. Sam is exercising his toes back and forth, his shoes sliding with the flow.

The door opens by a couple holding the leash of a German Shephard who starts barking and pulling the leash to smell Sam's legs. Sam reaches over to pet the dog, and the owner pulls him back as they approach the window.

"Sorry." The man says. "We can't do a thing with her. She needs to be put down."

Hearing the remark, Sam declares, "What? Why? How old is she?"

"Three, going on eighteen."

"It's a beautiful dog," Fran says. "I'm sure somebody would love to have it."

They hear the clerk telling them. "We'll take care of it for you." The door opens, and the man pulls the resisting dog barks at Sam.

"Fran, did you see that? That dog smelled King on my trousers."

Then the door opens from the inside, and Meredith comes to greet her mother and Sam. "Mom, what's on your mind? Hi Samuel."

"You got a few minutes?" Fran says. She relates to Meredith how they met George and Jimmy and their wives as they pulled into a spot in front of the diner, and it's no longer a secret. The entire town will know within a few days. So I had to come and tell you before you hear it from somebody else."

"Ah, that's great, Mom, and thanks. Harry and I can't keep it a secret either. It's all over the school. Even the principal approached us about it. So, we decided to officially announce it Monday.

During all this, Sam was thinking about the dog. *Should I or shouldn't I. The sheriff jokingly said King needed a mate just as I was to get one. Lord, are you leading me in this direction? Will Fran okay this or resist? And what about King? How will he react? Here I am. Have never wanted another pet to take care of, and one comes in here, the same kind as King. At this particular time, when the owners want to put their dog down. Lord, is this your doing? What am I to do? Will you Lord, give me a sign, a yes or a, no, do not get the dog.*

"Sam, did you hear Meredith? We've decided we'll tell them at church tomorrow. Are you okay with that?"

No response from Sam.

"Sam!"

"Huh? What?" he asks.

"You dreaming? Meredith and I agreed to announce our engagements in church."

"Yeah, sure. Let's get it over with."

Fran stands and hugs her daughter and tells her they're going to have dinner at Sams. Fran reaches down, grabs Sam's hand, leads him toward the door when he resists, and goes to the clerks' window. He leans over and says, "do not put the dog down. I may want it."

"Sam, honey. Did I hear you right, that you want that dog? Isn't one enough? They're not little puppies that sit in your lap. And you said the dog smelled King on your trousers. You wouldn't have let him pee on them, would you?

"Yeah, No! But he sure likes to rub against my legs. The dog smelled King, and that's what attracted her to me. Their sense of smell is, well, way above our ability. Right now, I don't know. I prayed about it, so let's wait."

He opens the door for Francinea, and he gets in the driver's seat, and off they quietly ride through the town, noticing the parked cars, folks strolling the sidewalks, and two older gentlemen in fur caps and jackets playing a board game. He passes the hardware store, where he sees a posted advertisement. "Yes, do it," in large type and the rest barely discernable. Reaching his mailbox, he slowly drives down the dirt road and stops in front of the porch. King comes running and barking out of the western woods.

Exiting the car, Sam hugs and pets his dog. "Hey buddy, would you like a friend to play with? The dog barks twice. "Hmm, was that a double yes? You want two?"

He and Fran enter the cabin, followed by King, who goes directly to his food bowl.

Fran pushes the closet curtain aside bends over to grab a sack of potatoes, an onion, a pepper, and some sauce. As the stove warms from the added wood, Sam is dressing down the trout, then pumping water into a pot on the stove for the potatoes, and all to cook, as Fran watches nearby.

"How your grandmother managed this through the years baffles me," Fran says. "Sam, at times, I think I could easily adjust, but then considering the abrupt change from easy cooking to this, I begin to think, what am I getting into?"

Sam continues with the food preparation while periodically testing the surface of the stove for hotness. "Another five minutes, and it'll be ready," Sam says. "Fran, did I hear you right? Are you second-guessing the move here? You're not getting cold feet, are you?"

"I don't know. It's such a drastic change."

Sam looks and feels under the table to confirm his idea is working. He looks at Fran. "You think I haven't had second thoughts? But, oh boy, that first month, I flunked the test in more ways than not. I screamed, why did I do this? It's tough, beyond my abilities. Why can't I have a microwave and buttons for lights, a computer and all? When I felt that way, I had to get out. I'd take a walk through the woods with

King. In that quietness of sitting in the grass and just looking around, my mind seemed to go somewhere else—the wonders of life and how it came to be dominated my thoughts. No way could it be just random bumping." Sam pauses. "But still, the difficulty of daily life stayed, and I envisioned Abe Lincoln in his log home, sitting next to the fireplace using a candle to read by. He did it, and so did millions. Somehow, I started to enjoy the learning process, and then slowly, the hardness of life without tech faded away. Fran, it's going to be the same with you, but you'll have me continually at your side. All I had was King's bark."

"Thanks," Fran says. "To all of us in town, it looked like you easily slid into your grandfather's steps, like one, two, three, go." She pauses and leans on his shoulder. "I'm okay. Now, Sam, my dear, what about the other dog?"

He whispers to her. "We've got to watch what we say in here. The FBI guy put a mike under the table. Everything is being recorded. But I think I've taken care of that."

"What? A mike to record our conversations?" She says.

"Yes. I'll inform the sheriff in church. Now, let's enjoy our dinner." They walk back in, and Fran asks again about the dog.

"Didn't you hear me ask about the dog? Are you, or not?"

"What do you think?"

"It's up to you."

"Nah, one King is good, but two, no. I did get something else."

"What's that?"

Fran's cellphone rings. She looks at it and pushes the green light. "Hello, Susan. How you doing?" She listens for a minute and replies, "That's great Sue. It all worked out."

Listening again to Susan as Sam watches her facial expressions go from a smile to raising her eyebrows. "Sue, thanks for calling, and again for your surprise visit. Blessings to you. Yes, we'll keep in touch. Good bye."

"So, they made it home and everything worked out," Sam says.

"Yes it did. Insurance provided a rental car and they made it home safely. Sam, I'm tired. It's been a full day, so I'm going home and rest."

"Our dinner? It's ready."

"Sorry hon, but I'm worn out. Too much for one day."

"It's ready now. Take some home to eat." Sam puts the trout, potatoes, and string beans in a covered sack. "Here. And blessings to you. Get that rest, and I'll see you tomorrow."

Seven

Sunday morning comes, and after his waking up routine, Sam gets ready for church.

On the walk to get the truck out of the barn, Sam sees that another couple of inches of snow fell last night. He tells his pet, "No, King, you're staying here." King bows his head, stretches his front paws over the fresh snow, lies down, looks up at Sam.

He starts the pick-up and lets it warm before backing out into the fresh snow. He hears a set of tires skidding to a stop.

"It's Fran."

Sam hurries to greet her.

"Good timing,"

"And, a good morning to you," Fran tells him. "You're looking super good. Thanks for dressing up for our announcement."

"Oh, do I need a tie?"

"No, that sweater will do just fine. So, hon, have you rehearsed what you'll say to everyone?"

"Me? I thought it was your job, my queen, the one who protects the king."

"No, seriously, have you?"

"Yes, dear. It's all right here." He points to a spot above his ear as he leans over to kiss his bride-to-be.

"You drive," Fran says.

"All I'm gonna say is, you accepted my proposal. Then I'll call Harry and Meredith to come up and let Harry make his announcement. After the boos and such, we'll announce it as a mother-daughter wedding ceremony on New Years Day."

"That's it?"

"Yeah, the pastor should announce it. But we'll see when we get there and hopefully have a chat with him."

"Hurry, then. We must get there while the pastor is still outside greeting everyone." Sam puts his foot down hard on the gas pedal, and they quickly cover the three miles to the church in the town square. He finds an open parking spot, and hand in hand, they walk toward the front door.

Pastor Thomas greets them. "Congratulations. Meredith informed me of your intentions last night at the youth banquet. So, I've arranged a time when we'll make the announcement. We've reserved the front pew for you. Your daughter is already there. At the time, I'll call you up to the stage. Then I'll spread the good news. Sam, I may ask you to say a few words. Is that okay?"

"Yes, sounds good," Fran answers. "He's always ready to talk."

"If there's anything else you want the church to know, write it down and hand it to the usher. Go on in."

They leave the pastor to finish his greeting time. Fran leads Sam down the center aisle to the first pew to greet and hug Meredith and Harry.

"Mom, guess what? Harry got the call from the University of Colorado. So that's settled."

"Oh, that's great."

"Yes, and closer to home, so that's where I'm applying."

Sam leans over to congratulate, "Good work Harry. Have you decided on a major?"

"Not yet, but carpentry as my minor."

"It'll come to you." Sam sees the pastor opening the door. He leans over to Fran and says, "If he asks me to say something about my history, you know me, I'll start yacking and yacking, so squeeze my hand."

The pianist plays a hymn as Pastor Thomas rushes onto the stage. "Good morning," he starts. "Glad to see you all this morning after getting a foot of snow with more on the way. But we are safe and sound under the mighty wonderful watchfulness of our God. Let us begin with our moment of silent worship. The pastor kneels by the altar, and the pianist softens the play. The congregation lower their heads. Husbands and wives hold hands, or embrace. It's quiet, except for softly mumbled prayers and praise.

A few minutes later, the pastor rises and announces, "Hymn 36." They find the hymn in the book and sing along with the worship leader.

After the ten-fifteen minute singing time, the pianist stops as Pastor Thomas returns to center stage. "I wish to break away from the usual practice this morning to make a few announcements of joy and blessings. Samuel Guardyall is a newcomer to our town, having joined us a few months ago. Come on up here, Samuel." Sam steps onto the stage to a round of applause.

"Samuel was gifted that log cabin by his grandfather, Joshua, who passed into glory two years ago." The pastor looks at Sam for reactions, then continues. "We've witnessed that he has become a replica of his grandfather in so many ways. He moved here to escape the continual loneliness of losing his wife. He related to me that the sorrow was more than he could bear. He took a drink, then another, and more to drown away the sorrows day by day for two months. Then one Sunday afternoon, he was watching a football game with a six-pack of beer beside him; a picture his wife had hung over the TV captured his attention. It was a painting of Jesus hanging on the cross. He described it this way to me: 'It seemed to come alive. He said he saw the droplets of blood pouring out of his sides, his forehead, all over that body. Each droplet exploded into a scene of him committing sins, such as stealing a package from a store and the lies he told in U-tube videos. He saw the lips of Jesus move. 'Son, I forgive you. Come unto me, and I will be with you and guide you hour by hour." Right there in his living room, Sam fell to his knees, cried out for forgiveness, and turned his life over to the Lord."

Pastor Thomas looks at Sam. "And, we have another member relatively new to us, Doctor Francinea Ingersall. Come up and join Samuel." The applause is louder as Fran stands next to Sam.

"These two are here to make an announcement. Sam, it's all yours."

Taking his hands out of his pockets, Sam says, "Thank you. A day or so later, I returned to work. I received a legal document informing me that my grandfather, whom I had never met, willed his cabin to me. So here I am seven months later. This is a wonderful town with unbelievable residents, so friendly and loving. I don't ever wish to leave. After a few months, an accident put me in the hands of Dr. Ingersall, who repaired my leg. From that first glance, she had my attention. She doesn't practice medicine. She does it exceedingly well. One day not long ago, she agreed to go fishing with me. I was enjoying her company more than throwing the hook and hope it catches a big trout. It was a beautiful fall day. The sun was warming us. The lake was calm, like a mirror reflecting the scenery of those massive mountains. Suddenly there was a jerk on her line. Yes, on her line, not mine! She pulled it in. The biggest rainbow trout I've ever seen. I was amazed. This amateur caught and reeled it in like a professional. Right there and then, I knew, I knew. I knew. I was on my knees in that rowboat and made the request. She said yes. So, a wedding celebration is coming."

Loud applause erupts through the sanctuary as everybody stands, shouting and cheering. Then, after a few moments, the applause quiets down to the pastor's raised arm.

"And, now, I want Francinea's daughter Meredith to join us. Harry, you too.

Applause starts again as they step onto the stage. Meredith steps into her mother's embrace.

A few high school friends yell out, "atta boy Harry! Yahoo!"

"You know Harry, a senior high school student with a B plus grade point along with being a star on the football team. He has now accepted a scholarship to the U. of Colorado. Meredith has already begun a career in medical care, working part-time with our veterinarian. These two will graduate this coming May, and then, well, I'll let Harry tell us the rest of the story.

Harry straightens, adjusts his tie and collar. "Ah, but ah, how do I begin? A few weeks ago, Meredith invited me to dinner with her mother. The food was—uhm. I don't remember as nervous as I was. All I wanted to do that day was spend more time with her. Sitting at the table, I cut a chunk of the steak, chewed it, and then, hey, forget the food. I got on my knees, opened the box, and asked Meredith if she would."

Her mother was watching. "What are you waiting for? Say yes now!"

"So, Meredith and I are engaged. She and her mother want a mother-daughter ceremony. We're working on that. Possibly New Year's Day."

The audience stands and cheers, and the pianist starts playing joyful music. When the audience slowly quiets down, Two men walk up on the stage with four chairs placing them behind the pastor. The pastor then tells Sam, Frncinea, Harry, and Meredith to remain onstage as I present a short sermon this morning.

At the podium, Pastor Thomas opens the Bible. "Everyone, please stand and open your bibles to Romans Chapter Twelve." Harry and Meredith, along with Francinea, touch their cell phones a few times to read along. Sam leans over to see the scripture on Fran's phone as the pastor looks on. Then, seeing that all appear ready, the pastor starts.

"Romans 12 'I beseech you therefore, brethren, by the mercies of God, that ye present your bodies a living sacrifice, holy, acceptable unto God, which is your reasonable service. And be not conformed to this world: but be ye transformed by the renewing of your mind, that ye may prove what is that good, and acceptable, and perfect, will of God.'" (KJV)

"Samuel here has shown us by adjusting to life in a cabin without electricity that he is not conformed to this technological world, as the rest of us are. But, should we abandon all this tech world? By marveling at the various aspects of creation, Samuel's mind is being transformed and renewed.

He pauses a bit, looking around, and then: "Let us continue in Romans."

'For I say, through the grace given unto me, to every man that is among you, not to think of himself more highly than he ought to think; but to think soberly, according as God hath dealt to every man the measure of faith. For as we have many members in one body, and all members have not the same office: So we, being many, are one body in Christ, and every one members one of another. Having then gifts differing according to the grace that is given to us,'

"No, we do not need to disconnect from the web technology to have our lives transformed to prove what is the good and acceptable will of God over our lives. Concentrate now, um, on that last sentence. God has dealt each of us a uniquely personal gift. Francinea has the gift of doctoring our illnesses and physical hurts. Meredith is discovering her gift by ministering to our pet animals. And Harry here is advancing the gift of carpentry, using that football scholarship to achieve it. Yes, he visualized and constructed this podium. Those two were led by God, not the web, not technology, to recognize their particular gift and are now perfecting those innate gifts. All of us must do the same. We can use the web, but, um, don't let it use you. Let your mind be transformed and renewed, and then rule that web that's so tempting.

"There is much more for us in Romans twelve, but that's it for today. Now, let us gather together in our fellowship hall for a luncheon dinner worthy of celebrating the future of these four members."

He leads Fancinea and Samuel, Meredith, and Harry down the aisle to the congregation's high fives and hand shakings.

"Sheriff Olsen, oh, how great it is to see you," Samuel says as they enter the room.

"Come here, Fran. Again, congratulations," the sheriff tells her.

They hug, and Fran tells him that Sam is acting like a ruler King."

The sheriff looks at Sam, removes his nightstick, and puts it into Sam's side. "Sam, what'll I do to straighten you out?"

"Come, join us. Now, remember, the king rules overall, and that includes you, sheriff. After this, you've got to join us in the cabin, and you'll see where this cousin thought came from."

The sheriff replies. "You said there was more about the demise of the previous sheriff."

"Yes, that too."

"I'll bring my wife out. She's helping in the kitchen."

"Sheriff, there's something else there. And I hope you can take care of it."

"What's that, Sam?"

Looking around, Sam tells the sheriff about the microphone the FBI guy put under his kitchen table."

"Oh no."

"I have muzzled it temporarily. I've read the constitution, and it clearly states freedom of speech is protected, so can't we use that?"

"Let me think it through. Now it's time to relax and enjoy the fellowship." The sheriff says and leaves to find his wife.

Sam and Francineau, with Meredith and Harry, join the others waiting in line. The dinner time passes as they chop down on the BBQ ham, turkey, and beef along with baked potatoes, celery, and choice of iced water, Pepsi, or coffee. Many church members visit their table with best wishes and questions.

The football coach congratulates Harry on getting the scholarship. "You'll do great. It's a school the pros watch the games for possible drafts, so be aware of that possibility."

Harry replies, "I don't want to go that route. From what I've heard, I'd be turning my life over to them. Like being in the military. I'd rather have my own woodworking business."

After dinner, Sam, driving Fran's car with Harry and Meredith in the rear seats, go to the cabin to relax and re-evaluate their New Year's Day plans.

"Mom," Meredith says, "the principal told us he was called by the State telling him that no married teen students are allowed to attend high schools in the state."

"That's baloney! You can and you will." Francinea states. "How did they find out about it?"

"Well," Merideth begins. "I got curious about marriage and school and wanted to see if other students had completed school while married. So, I searched the web to see if there was anything about eighteen-year-old married students continuing high school. I found one site, and all it indicated was that it was in the state and the principal's hands. Whatever they decided."

Sam, hearing this explanation says, "Whoever that was, collected your information off your computer and forwarded it to the Colorado Board of Education for them to investigate. I was able to get all sorts of information off the web about possible firms to do the work. It's easy to download personal information."

"Sam, what can they do if the principal denies their student status?" Fran asks.

"Home online classes."

Sam then adds, "Hey, on Monday, let's go to the library, use their computer and search for those online classes. You both know what courses you need for graduation, right?"

"Yeah," Harry says. He looks over at Meredith. "Yes, at two-thirty, we can. The football season will be over, so I'd be free from that. Yes, Meri, let's do it."

"Oh, Sam. Thanks." Fran grabs his arm. "How do you do it? You've got an answer for everything."

"I'm the king, remember." Fran punches his belly, and King, sitting at Sam's feet, rises and barks at her. Sam places his hand between Fran and the dog's nose. "King, stop it!"

"Hmm?" Sam says. "That's the first time he's done anything like that. Hmm? You think he's getting jealous? Perhaps I should get that dog."

There's a knock on the door, it opens, and the sheriff and his wife Marjorie enter. "We're not breaking in on personal time, are we?" Sheriff Olsen says and rubs King's neck and down his back as his wife looks around the cabin.

"No, no! Good timing," Sam replies. He stands and gets two folding camp chairs out of the closet, placing them next to the couch by the fireplace.

"Marjorie, how are you doing?" Fran says.

"Doing okay. Thanks. The last time I was here was when Amilia held a cooking class. That was in June, like three or four years ago."

"If you ever want to find something or someone, Marg can do it."

Sam, Harry, Meredith, and Francinea look at each other, causing the sheriff to ask, "what'd I say to get that look?"

"Oh, nothing," Sam answers. "About that mike. I put a pack of bread dough over it. Will that stop it?"

"Bread dough?"

"Yeah. About three inches thick. I thought that would muffle it. So, we've been freely talking. Come on over and take a look. What else can we do?"

The sheriff looks at the microphone and pulls it away. He removes the dough. Turns the recording devise over to Inspect it. Holding it close, he says, "This is Sheriff Bill Olsen of Johnsonville County, Colorado. By placing and hiding this device in the home of a private citizen, whoever you are, you have violated his private personal rights. As the sheriff, I have the right and duty to confiscate this invasive equipment. It will be in my office. The state office will be informed. Good-bye." The sheriff removes two screws on its backside and removes the batteries. "Here's a couple of batteries for you, Sam. When I get to the office in the morning, I'll take it apart and may be able to hear what was transmitted and to whom. That information is on the disk."

"Yahoo Thanks, sheriff." Sam shakes his hand. "Now, I see that Fran has Marjorie looking through the journal you came to see. Go over and get informed."

Meredith gets up from her seat on the couch, so the sheriff can sit next to his wife.

"Where's the write-up about the previous sheriff?"

"Skim through to 1962."

After reading those notes, the sheriff says, "Since we talked about this, I did some further research. The Johnsonville County News had an article about it later that year indicating the sheriff had been kidnapped, stabbed, drowned in alcohol, and put in that ditch by a government agent, who later confessed and sentenced to life imprisonment. A year later, the paper stated that the man escaped prison and is living somewhere. Nobody knows where. At the end of the article, The FBI indicated the man was a Russian communist. In 1962? I was just six," the sheriff adds. I don't remember much at all. The dinners at the church, and I remember standing in the backyard watching these people riding horses through the woods. Oh, these notes bring back memories I hadn't thought about for years. And yes, we are cousins from three generations in the past."

"Turn back to 1941.

December 8, 1941

Oh, we're mourning over the news. The Japanese bombed Pearl Harbor. Two young men from Johnsonville were there on another ship. They are okay. The town held a prayer meeting for our brave men. Joshua is safe as he was in Air force training in Colorado Springs. He enlisted in October.

Sam says. "That's my grandfather."

"How long did he serve the country?" Fran asks.

"I don't know. He survived the war somehow. Where and how, who knows. These notes skip through time like a Doe jumping fences. Back in '36, there's a couple notes that caught me."

August 30, 1936

Our pastor had gathered the flock together and prayed a blessing on our future safety. No more hail storms damaging the area.

September 15

Joshua, now 12, wants his own horse. He doesn't like the walk to school. Samuel then told him to build a carriage, and when that's done, we'll see.

After this, Marie wrote hardly anything informative until the late '50s. Just things about the garden and cooking. Why? Surely, there were other events in those years worth writing a note, a one, two-liner. But that's it, my cousin."

The sheriff grins and firmly says, "So Sam, you're also just like everyone else I have to keep an eye on. It does not give you any special privileges, so watch it."

"Got it. I've got a horse now just like my grandfather, so I won't be speeding on YOUR roads."

"Sam, honey, you got a horse? You never told me you were going to get a horse."

"When Mark and Susan were, I said I was thinking about it."

Fran replies, "thinking and doing are two very different actions."

"Friday, I said I would have a big surprise for you on Saturday. But you went to help those homeless kids, so we didn't get to talk about it. And yesterday in the cabin, I was about to, but that call from Susan interrupted.

"Do you have a horse, or are you joking again?"

"Yes, I do. No joke. The guy brought it over yesterday morning while you were working."

"This, I gotta see—you, riding a horse?"

"Sure, right now. Let's all go to the barn. You'll also see the carriage I've been updating. He opens the barn door, and the horse is in the first stall chewing on hay. Sam hooks up the head halter, slides the bit into the horse's mouth, and tightens the straps. He rubs the horse's back a few times, throws a blanket over its back, then a saddle, and buckles the loop around the belly. He tests the tightness and steps into the stirrup, and up he goes.

Francinea quietly watches.

"Giddy up." Sam pulls on the reins and goes bouncing toward the gazebo with King running and barking alongside.

Harry starts clapping and shouting, "show'em, cowboy."

Sam guides the horse toward them. "I'm going to go check the mailbox." And up the dirt road, he goes out of sight with King barking up a storm.

Meredith puts her arm around her mother, "what you thinking?"

"I don't know."

"I think it's a great idea." Her daughter comforts. "You saw the carriage. Imagine the joy of riding in that through town. Even now, with cold weather, wrapped up nice and cozy in a blanket breathing the fresh air. Oh, mom, that's a scene right out of Hollywood."

Fran looks at her daughter.

The sheriff says, "Reminds me of his grandparents. They would do that on Sunday morning for church. Hey, Fran, I'm sure you noticed a few spots in town that still has posts to tie horses to."

"That's what those posts are for?"

Margorie moves in close to Fran. "Bill has told me that Sam had been thinking of a horse ever since he moved in. He just never got around to it. He had too many other things to learn. The carriage is beautiful, and you'll love it. I can see you there cuddled up next to Sam under a blanket, leaning on his shoulder and resting all your cares away."

"Oh, thank you." Fran brings Marjorie and Meredith in a good hug.

The horse and King come into view without Sam.

"Now, what happened?" Fran wonders. Soon, Sam is seen limp walking down the path. Fran and all run to him. "What happened? Are you okay?"

"Yeah, I'm okay. Dang horse does not know that when I say stop, he's supposed to stop."

"You're limping. Did he throw you? You fall off? What?"

"Ah, I decided to walk alongside for a bit, when he just started to run, and I yelled Stop. I started running after it and tripped over a branch or something. Oh, he's gonna learn English: stop, go, left, right."

Harry and the sheriff softly chuckle as Fran inspects his hip and leg.

Sam looks around, "Where is he?"

"The horse is in the barn," the sheriff tells Sam. "King got the loose reins and led him into the stall. This has been an interesting afternoon. Margy, we must go. Sam, you can get a nice hat in Johnsonville, along with the chaps and boots. Take care. Fran and Meredith, I admire you both for your convictions and upcoming celebrations. And Harry, keep your eyes on the path, and you'll get your desires. We'll see ya."

Marjorie tells Fran, "the boss says we must go, we go, so blessing to you all. Sam that journal Amila left is a treasure. I think I might be framing and hanging them for sweet-time memories."

"Bye, sheriff. Thanks for everything." Sam says. "Oh, almost forgot. Cousin Bill."

"Sam," Fran says. "Let's go in the cabin, and I'll take a look at your hip."

"Hmm? What else would you like to see?"

"Oh, I'll see you all right. Begging the queen for forgiveness." Fran massages his leg and around his sore hip with her gentle medicinal touches. "Ah, you'll be fine." She hesitates and directly peers into his eyes, takes a deep breath. "Sam, I thought we had agreed to talk our choices, everything over together. And now you buy a horse without telling me. I don't know."

Eight

Sam wakes up early this Monday morning. He opens the bottom section of the dutch door to let King out and feels the cold air breeze up his pajama legs. He fires up the stove and the fireplace. While rubbing his hands together over the new flames, he says, "And this is just the beginning of winter. Oh, why? Ah, complaining again. Stop it!"

Pouring himself a glass of orange juice, some thoughts come. *No big deal announcements party for thanksgiving. Just standard family time.* He dresses for the weather, takes the banana and coffee to the deck, and finds his pet there licking his paws. "Hey King, shall we go for a ride? Or, a walk?"

Sam and the dog slowly walk through the western woods toward the stream. He pauses as the sight of ducks resting in some open waters gets his attention. *Does Thanksgiving always require a turkey? Grandma has a recipe in the closet for how she handled thanksgiving."* Sam and the dog finish the half-hour trek and return to the cabin. He refreshes his cup of coffee, sits on the couch by the fireplace with his grandmother's recipes. He jots down the finer points, the ingredients and makes a list of items to get.

At the typewriter, he starts.

MY Cabin Life 20

Here it is Monday, with thanksgiving three days away. Our big planned engagement announcements at thanksgiving got canceled. Well, not canceled, as in no engagements, but moved up to yesterday in church. So now, we, the four of us, will have the traditional family Thanksgiving here in this cabin.

Thinking of this brings back beautiful memories of past turkey dinners. As a kid of eight or ten, mom prepared it all. As poor as we were, I wondered then, why, how did she get all this extra good stuff. She said she wanted me to have it all on this special day. She held my hands and prayed. She then told me about that original Thanksgiving. Oh, her way of telling stories was fantastic. I always wanted to hear more, but on that particular day, she said, 'enough, let's enjoy this time together. We are so blessed to be here in America. And you will be rich someday, so work hard, keep doing it, and you will make me proud.'

Oh, the food was so good, I managed to hide pieces of it in my pockets. It was just mom and me as dad had left. Her parents were off across the country somewhere. No sisters, no brothers nearby, just us.

I had to walk a mile to get to school. While the other kids were eating lunch, I made an excuse to practice throwing the ball at the square I drew on the wall and later became the pitcher on the high school and then a college team.

Somehow, mom came and watched every game. Now, in this memory bank, I see her sitting in the first row, smiling when I did good and frowning when I threw a bad pitch. And then, two months before I graduated college, she suddenly got sick and passed on to glory. Sitting at her bedside, she told me she'd be watching and then jumping with joy when I got that degree that would lead me to riches and fame. Her last words to me were: 'Don't give in. Do it.'

Yes, Thanksgiving. Do we try to put ourselves in there alongside those first settlers after such a long tiring ocean trip and thrilled to be in this new land. Then sickness devastated them to wonder was it worth it? Why did we do this? So far away.

Yet, they lifted their hands to heaven, thanking God for their blessings in this new land of everything. They kept at it. They had to. They worked hard, plowing the ground and reaping a harvest. Turkey, corn, beans, potatoes, onions, peppers, and tomatoes, and a choice of pies or cake for dessert. Oh, the joy of it all must have been overwhelming. So wonderous, it was written down on parchment to keep for memories.

And here we are just a few hundred years later, and we quick and easily get everything at a store, not thinking nor even wondering how it all got on the shelves.

And now, I am faced with that special day coming when I must do it. Initially, Fran said she could do it at home, and she and Meredith would bring it all. But something inside leads me to do it and learn the old-fashioned way. The pilgrims did it. Abe Lincoln and his wife did it. Grandma and pa did it. Those recipes, the methods are right here in front of me. Follow the directions. How hard can that be?

So, yes, when Fran stops here this evening, I will tell her. Oh, yes. The roe over the recent purchase of the horse seemed to upset her. Yes, I Will straighten all this out with Fran this evening.

Sam pulls the sheets out of the typewriter and slides them in the drawer with the others. He gets ready for the trip to the grocery store. He starts the pick-up to warm as he clears the windows of any snow or ice. King jumps onto the seat, barking at the closed window. "No, I'm not opening the window." He backs out of the barn and heads out to the main road. In the store, he grabs a cart and starts collecting the items on his grandmothers' list. At the rear of the store, he ponders the fresh items in the refrigerated case.

"Samuel, good to see you, and congratulations." Paul, the owner of the store, says from behind the case of various meats.

"Hey, Paul. Thanks. No turkeys in there."

"Sold out. More coming later today. Meredith got our last one an hour or so ago."

"Meredith did?"

"Yes, Sam. Is that a problem?"

"Oh! No. What time will the turkeys arrive?"

"They're flying in from Nebraska. So, about three or four."

"Thanks, Paul. Save one for me."

Paul slides over to help another customer.

Sam looks down at his full cart, wondering. *Meredith got a turkey. I'm gonna have one. Is she and Fran still thinking of doing it all and then bringing it out? Must straighten this out this evening.*

Sam continues his shopping, loads it in the truck's bed, and heads to the cabin. He carries the five sacks inside and separates the items on the butcher block table, putting some in the icebox.

"I'll get a block of ice this afternoon."

Sam sits on the couch to digest the Thanksgiving day feast preparations again after adding more wood to the stove and fireplace. *Okay, the turkey is first. Grandma said that one year they had ten from the church. She cooked two medium-sized turkeys—one in the stove and the other over the embers of the fireplace.*

At two-thirty, Sam heads out for town and stops at the grocery store first. "Afternoon Paul." Sam greets the owner behind the glass case.

"Got it for you, Sam. A twelve-pounder, wrapped and ready." Paul answers as he puts the package on the counter.

"Twelve? That's a medium?" Sam exclaims as he picks it up.

"Yep, the same size as your grandmother always wanted. Anything bigger would not fit inside that stove of yours."

"Wow! What're the biggest ones like?"

"Oh, they go up to twenty to twenty-two pounds. Sam, this is your first time at this, right?"

"Yes, it is."

"Ah, excuse me a minute. "Mrs. Slantin, how can I help you today?"

"Paul, give me three of those prime steaks, please. Individually wrapped." She looks at Sam, "Mr. Guardyall, that Frasncinea of yours let my husband die on the operating table."

"What? She let your husband die?"

"Yes, he was in for a check-up, and she opened him up and left him for the nurses. She told me there was nothing she could do. It was too advanced."

"Oh, I'm so sorry. How long ago was that? He had cancer?"

"Six-seven months."

"I'm sorry. I'm sure Fran did all she could. Would you mind if I prayed for you now?"

"Pray? Ha. That's a joke." She spits on the floor in front of Sam, grabs the steaks from Paul, and leaves.

Standing dumbfounded, Sam looks back at Paul, who shrugs his shoulders. Sam hurries through the store, pays for the turkey, leaves, and looks around for any sign of the lady. He starts the truck, backs up, and slowly drives down Main street. "Oh, Lord God, please bless Mrs. Slantin. Somehow minister to her. Bring peace to her soul." He stops at the Ice plant and takes home a ten-pounder. On the road back to the cabin, he tells himself: "I must ask Fran about this when she stops this evening."

After placing the block of ice, he warms his coffee. Knowing that he has about two hours until Fran leaves work, he selects a book from his grandfather's collection. He relaxes on the couch with 'The City of God' by St. Augustine. Every couple of minutes, he quits rubbing the back of his pet to turn the page. *Fascinating! Here we are, modern people, some 1600 years later, and we're experiencing the same type of conflicts between Christians and the state he witnessed and described as typical in the fifth century.*

Periodically, he looks up at the clock and back to the book, which has captured his curiosity—slowly reading to digest the thoughts, time slips by when he finally peeks at the clock.

"Wow? It's six-thirty. Where's Fran?" He bookmarks the page in Chapter three and goes outside waiting on Fran. "Oh, I've got to get that cell phone. She could call to let me know, or I could call." He waits. He sips his coffee. He pets the dog. He prays. He wonders: *where is she? She always stops here after work. She wouldn't skip and go home. Was she held up working late? An emergency operation? I can't leave, she may show up then. Oh, Lord, if only I had your vision of everything, I'd know, I'd see what's happening. I could comfort her. I wouldn't be wondering.*

"Stop it!" Sam tells the air. "King, let's take a walk to the road." He slides his hands into the gloves, adjusts his cap and scarf, Grabs the flashlight, and follows the dog passing the barn, the garden area, around the bend, following the beam of the flashlight into the tree-lined road leading up to the main highway between Prairieville and Johnsonville. They reach his mailbox and the shuttered fruit stand. He waves at a car passing by. He reaches down for a fist full of snow, rolls it around, and throws it into the trees for King to run after in the light of the flashlight. He's got another one ready. Tail wagging King approaches and sees the white ball flying over his head. King turns and runs to catch it. Watching King, he hears a car honking its horn and blinking its headlights as it passes by. Too quick to recognize who it was. Another one from Johnsonville passes quickly. He pats together another snowball, and this time, he throws it down his road. "Okay, boy, back we go." Shining the light in front of King, he follows the dog back to the cabin to warm up and eat something. On the way, he says, "Even though I vowed against submitting to these modern wonders, I think that tomorrow, I will get that cell phone. It's become imperative."

Nine

"King! Get off me!" Sam screams as his pet suddenly lands on Sam's back and pushes a paw across his cheek. The dog continues to make Sam aware of his need to find a tree. Sam throws the blanket over the dog, rolls out of bed, and jumps as his feet touch the cold floor. "Out you go," Sam declares as he opens the door for King.

Sam puts sticks and logs over the embers in the fireplace. He does the same to the oven and lights his Coleman stove to heat the coffee. He tosses the curtain aside, gets, peels, and chews a banana as he dresses warm for the morning. As the coffee is brewing, he looks out the frosted window over the sink. "Today is the day."

Carrying the cup of coffee to the couch, he settles in for his devotional time when he hears the barking and sees King's face through the window over the desk. "Okay." He goes to let his pet in from the cold. With King at his side on the couch, he opens the Bible to the bookmarked page in 2 Corinthians 6. He stops at verse 17. *Hmm? Am I about to touch the unclean thing by getting a cell phone? How does one know for sure? Paul is writing this two thousand years ago to the people of Corinth, imploring them to put away the earthly yokes of the unbelievers. If these cell phones had been available back then, would Paul be carrying one wherever he went? The cabin and this way of life sure is separated from the rest of the world. Right? I acquiesced when I got the Coleman camp stove. Is the cell phone another inch closer to full throttle? Nope, it won't be. I'm going to get one. Today. This Morning.*

He bows his head, praying out loud, "Lord, is a cell phone an unclean thing in this now world? Everyone has one. I'll keep it clean. It's just an object for communication with friends, etcetera."

He continues reading. An hour later, he's dressed for the ride to Johnsonville. He parks the truck near the superstore, walks inside, looks around, and heads to the electronics section.

"No, sir, we don't have that kind of phone here. This one is similar but so much more convenient and useful."

"Sheriff Olsen said I could get one here. He called it a dumb phone."

"Oh, that one," the young man says. He points to a package hanging on a hook. Sam reads about the phone, turns the package over to read the directions.

"Okay. I'll take it." He pays the clerk. In the truck, he unpacks the phone, inserts the battery, and presses the button to watch the green circle go round and round. He punches the sheriff's number. "Hello, sheriff, this is Sam. I just got a phone, so I wanted to call and let you know my number." He listens for a bit and says, "Thanks, goodbye."

Now Fran. No, I shouldn't. She may be involved in surgery or loafing in the office. He backs up and starts the short drive to the hospital. At a stoplight, he hears someone calling his name. He rolls down his window and shouts, "Hey, Gene."

"Sam, wow! you're just the one I was looking for."

"Huh?"

"Yeah, you doing anything?" The light turns green, and Gene says, "Pull into the parking lot, Sam." Gene is right behind him. He gets out of his car and tells Sam, "I signed up to play in the Old Rascals Invitational. We need a fourth. It'll be Paul from the grocery store, Pastor Thomas, you and me. The sheriff couldn't make it. Something came up."

"Gene, no classes today?"

"It's Thanksgiving week. Come on, join us."

"I haven't played for a year. I sold my clubs."

"No problem. We'll get you a set at the clubhouse. Come on. It'll be fun. You got nothing else to do, do you? It's a scramble format."

Sam looks at his watch, thinking of Fran and when she'd be free.

"But the weather. It's cold, and it snowed the other day."

"Ah, so what? A new experience. We'll have a heater in the cart. We'll finish the round about two and then hear about the new Young Rascals Ministry. It's a fund-raising event. Come on, Sam, join us. The pastor and Paul are in our group?"Yes. Meeting you here has been divine. I know it. Follow me."

Sam follows him out of town. They turn left into the golf course's parking lot.

"Thank You, Lord," Sam tells the air as he gets out of the car.

In the clubhouse, Gene introduces Sam to Jack Smith, the pro. "He needs a good set of clubs. He sold his before moving into the cabin."

"Ah," the pro says, "You're the guy who's living in Joshua's cabin. Welcome." He calls out to a clerk. "Bring a set of the Palmer Special for Mr. Guardyall."

"You knew my grandfather?" Sam asks Jack.

"Oh, yes. He's the one who got me interested in golf. It was at a scout camp out at the cabin. I was ten or eleven. We were messing around while the scoutmaster and your grandfather were watching. I found a limb to hit rocks into the lake. Joshua brought me a five-iron and three balls. Hitting those balls into the lake was great. Watching me doing that, he said I had a natural swing and should take up the game. I was hooked."

"Wow," Sam says.

"Yeah, you never forget things like that. I couldn't thank him enough. I earned a scholarship to play for the Nebraska Warriors and later as a teaching pro. And here I am. Do you play much?"

Sam replies, "I used to in Indianapolis. When I turned fifty, I shot my age … on the front nine."

"I'll bet that was in the newspaper." Jack chuckles. The clerk brings the set of clubs. "Here you are. You've got time to hit a few at the range."

"Thanks."

"Go! Your group will tee off on the ninth. Have fun."

"Jack, anytime, you're welcome at the cabin. Bring your wife, and we'll have dinner together. Here's my phone number. Give me a call."

"Gene, wow! Unbelievable. Every day, I hear another fantastic bit about my grandparents and their life here."

Riding along the cart path to the range, Sam is warming his hands in front of the heater. Gene tells Sam that the sheriff called, wondering if we got a replacement. "He wished he was here to watch you play."

Sam replies, "I'm not sure I want to see me play."

They join Pastor Thomas and Paul at the range for a five-minute warm-up.

A siren blows. An announcer informs everyone to go to their assigned tee-boxes. "We'll tee off in ten minutes."

During the four-hour round, Paul informs Sam more about Mrs. Slantin. "She wouldn't accept the medical exam the hospital provided as fact and then started terrorizing Francinea with those insults. Fran's partner tried to get her to sue Mrs. Slantin for slander, but she wouldn't. The mayor tried to calm that lady down, as had the previous pastor. She's still at it."

Sam learns from Pastor Thomas that the previous pastor suddenly up and left without explanation six months ago. A month later, he was accepted and appointed as the church's pastor.

Playing a scramble relieved the pressure on Sam. He discovered that Gene just likes to get out in the fresh air, and whatever happens, happens. He hit three in the ponds. Pastor Thomas got to know more of each of them personally. He would periodically say things like, "Hallelujah. Thank You, Lord. Hey guys, it's just a game. Enjoy the time."

The time of play slows on the sixth hole as the team in front looks for balls in the tall grass.

Standing on the tee waiting, Sam opens the conversation. "This morning, I was reading Corinthians when I started to wonder how St. Paul managed to travel so far and write so much to so many without any of our conveniences. No texting messages. No car to drive. No restaurants, no restrooms on the trail. It boggles my mind every time I read about the ancients, what they did, and what they accomplished, like building the original Cathedral in Jerusalem, those colosseums in Greece seating thousands. The pyramids? All those huge multi-thousand-pound blocks, placed at a precise angle on top of others. How? Churches from the 4th and 5th centuries are still standing throughout Europe. No way could we, or would we even try to reconstruct one of those? And, yeah, to imagine myself with Moses, climbing that mountain and stay there for what was it, forty days. Food? Water? A shelter of some sort? No, I'd give in after two days, saying this is stupid. And now, well, we spend much of our time in entertainment. Golf is a great game, but compare this to fighting off a lion with only a shield and sword. Were those gladiators married? What were their wives and kids thinking?"

'Sam," Pastor Thomas says. "I believe God put you in that cabin for a purpose that's beyond making do without electricity. You've got a gift. Use it. What you said gets us all to think beyond our pleasant reality. I'd like to pursue this further sometime in the office or your cabin. Perhaps a bible study?"

Gene announces, "Time to hit the ball. Sam, you're up."

"This is a par five. We need to birdie this one," Sam states as he grips his driver. He swings and pow; the ball curves left, and bounces in the pond. "Ooops."

They ended up paring the hole as Paul's second shot rolled up to the edge of the green and then back into the low area. They three-putted from there.

"Two more to play and then the ceremony," Pastor Thomas says. "I've enjoyed it. Gene, thanks for thinking of me when you enrolled in this event."

They finish playing. Sam returns the clubs and bag to the pro shop, asking if he could see Mr. Smith.

"Sorry, he's on the practice tee with a student."

"The clubs were great. Thanks," Sam tells the attendant. "Have the pro cal mel sometime. He's got my number."

"I will, Mr. Guardyall."

Sam joins up with Gene, Paul, and the pastor in the banquet hall, along with the other sixty-some golfers sitting at round tables enjoying the hot drinks, chips, and barbequed chicken wings.

A twenty-something young man takes center stage.

"Well, how did you old rascals do out there?" he says. "First of all, my name is Jason Whoduhaha. Don't laugh. It's my Cheyenne heritage, and I'm proud of it and proud to be here. I wish to thank the organizers and the staff for their work in securing and preparing the Johnsonville golf course for this event. Yes, some snow was along a few fairway edges, but you managed by using red balls. Mostly the course was playable, thanks to the crew. The idea came about three months ago as my mentor, Doctor Johanson, proposed a ministry to help foster, and neglected children throughout the county, and beyond if necessary. It surprised me when he said there were hundreds of these youngsters in need in this county. Who would have suspected such a large number? I didn't, and I've lived here my twenty-five years. I guess that's a sign of how we live, centered on our own happiness and well-being.

"During high school and college, and in the seminary, I never imagined that so many children in the area needed basic help like a warm bed to sleep in, a decent meal, clothes, and shoes. Many get in trouble with the law and end up in jail. I interviewed a twelve-year-old kid in the county jail for stealing a ham sandwich from the deli. No one came to bail him out. He told me he gets to eat every day and has a cushion, a pillow, and a blanket on his bed in his own room."

'No big deal,' he said."

"We came up with the name Young Rascals for this ministry centered on finding, helping, and educating neglected children.

"Myself, I'm a recent graduate of the Northeast Colorado Reformed Church Seminary here in Johnsonville. My calling is the same as yours. Spread the Gospel. Help those in need. Do unto others as you would have them do to you. Let's do it."

He turns to look at a screen descending as the lights go off.

The audience sees a helicopter flying over the town, its main street, its western and eastern suburb-type residential areas. It circles the hospital and then follows the western road into the forested hills. The helicopter hovers. Then pictures on the screen show tents alongside a creek.

A voice declares, "That is a homeless camp. Without the scanning of helicopters, we would never know about those camps in these woods. When the plane landed, the crew of three hiked into the woods and found not just one but three tented camps. They couldn't believe what they were seeing. Three tents, ten kids, one adult. In the other camp. Six tents around a campfire, eight children, all under the age of ten, and one sixteen-year-old girl caring for those little kids. At another site, a half-mile away, were three men, not in tents but under a canvas tied to four trees. When our men approached the area, they ran across the creek and deep into the woods." He pauses to scan the audience for reactions.

"Horrifying, isn't it? To think, even imagine such a scenario in this age of plenty for all of us. Why?

"Now, I want to introduce you to a special woman who tripped over this a few weeks ago. She was doing her duties in the hospital when an announcement was notifying the EMR staff that two small children were abandoned at the emergency door. This lady rushed there and administered aid to those children. The parent was nowhere around.

"Doctor Francinea Ingersall, come on up here. Not only did this doctor minister to those two kids, but she investigated." Sam is astounded, seeing his future bride on the stage.

"Doctor Ingersall has agreed to tell the story."

"Thank you, Jason," Fran begins. "It's a privilege to be here and be able to relate this sad event. But first, you old rascals, you enjoyed having fun on the golf course today, so now, take out your wallets and be ready to give. Give big. This ministry needs it."

Fran sees Sam sitting at one of the tables in the second row. She smiles, and he returns the look.

Fran continues. "I was walking to the office after surgery when I heard that announcement. I peeked in the emergency room, where the nurses had two small boys, one about four years old and the other possibly three. They each had bloody streaks across their backs and the knuckles of their hands. They had been beaten, whipped by belts. The boys would not talk, nor were they crying in pain. We could not get their names or any other information from them. They simply would not speak. The nurses swabbed to get their DNA. The next day, I tried again to get them to at least say their names. Nope. They were scared.

"Doctor Johansen, who's retired and was putting this ministry together, offered to help. With his many contacts, he was able to locate the mother by the DNA of the kids. Three months previously, she had been released from prison in Nebraska on drug charges. During her two-year term, her mother took care of the boys. When she was released, she demanded custody of her children. She has now been arrested and locked up again, this time on child abuse reported by a neighbor. The two boys are back with their grandmother in LaPlatte, Nebraska, where they are loved and cared for. Hallelujah!

"So, you've heard some of what this ministry desires to correct—lost kids out of sight in this peaceful community. So give. No excuse from old rascals enjoying the good life. Dig deep."

Fran gives the microphone back to Jason Whoduhaha.

"Thank you, doctor. We've secured an old elementary schoolhouse where we intend to board any youngsters abandoned or neglected. All those kids we found living in tents are now in the safe confines of that building, bunkered down in two old classrooms—one for boys and another for the few girls. We intend to partition the large classrooms into several double occupancy private rooms. Your contributions to this ministry will enable us to do that along with other necessary physical changes. We desire to fence the playgrounds for some new slides and swings. There's also a ball diamond. Thank you so much for being so attentive. I will now turn this over to Doctor Johanson, the director of the ministry."

"Thank you, Jason. Now, I won't bother you with any other details. There would be too many, and I'd rather not repeat any of it. It depends on you. Will you help us to minister and care for these children and their needs. We have a full-time nurse, a volunteer donating her time in the kitchen preparing the meals for these children, and a janitor to keep the place clean.

"Jason has been fantastic. He has carpenters lined up to start the physical work of partitioning the rooms. He has plumbers ready to add more restrooms. All he needs is the funds to secure the materials to get started. Please, make checks out to The Young Rascals Program. An usher will be at the back where you can drop cash and/or the envelopes provided at each table. Thank You."

Sam picks up the envelope, reads the type, takes a pen, and indicates how much he intends to give. He stands and begins to follow the others out of the auditorium when Fran interrupts his walk. She throws her arms around his neck, plants a quick kiss saying, "Sam, honey, I didn't know you'd be here. I heard that Gene, Pastor Thomas, Paul, and the sheriff had signed up."

"Yeah, I didn't know either. The sheriff canceled, and Gene bumped into me on the road and asked if I'd be interested. Well, not if. It was a demand. So, here I am. Amazing day." He takes the cell phone out of his pocket. "Look what I got."

"You got a phone?"

"Yes, I did. I gave in and bought one. And that's why I was here in town where Gene found me."

She grabs the device out of his hand, unfolds it, presses a symbol, and sees just one contact, the sheriff. She enters her name and number. "There, now you've got my contact information." She pulls out her phone and records his number.

"Let's go eat. I'm in a mood for a good steak."

"Hey Gene," Sam hollers to get his attention. "If you hadn't stopped and yelled at me, I would've been in the cabin feeling lousy. You helped make my day. Thanks."

Gene replies. "I need to thank you for agreeing to this. Fran, you were great up there. Sam was all eyes and ears smiling joy when you stepped onto the stage."

"Where's King? Sam." Fran asks. "He's always with you."

"He's in the barn. This morning, I left him there to watch and be with the horse. I would not be here with you if I had King."

"Let's go then. I'll follow you to the restaurant." She takes his hand in hers as they walk to the parking lot.

Ten

"Ah, a bit cold out there, eh!" Sam tells his pet after opening the Dutch door to let him in. King licks and chews some delights.

"Woof! Woof!"

"Good, you like it. When you're finished with that, rest a bit, and then we're going for a ride." At the typewriter, Sam punches the keys.

A note to me on this Thanksgiving morning.

Sam finishes the brief note. He slides his feet into the snow boots, dons the hooded jacket, gets his gloves, and opens the door. King is right beside Sam walking to the barn. He bridles the horse and hooks it to the two-wheel-covered carriage with a two-person cushioned seat.

King jumps onto the seat next to Sam. "Wonder, let's go. Giddy up," he announces as he snaps the reins, and off they go. King barks at the horse as it trots out toward the road.

"Whoa there!" Sam says, pulling back on the reins as they approach the road. "Okay, giddy-up," he tells the horse, snapping the reins to his left. They're off to Prairieville and Fran's home. A mile or so from town, Sam hears a siren. He looks in the mirror and pulls on the reins to slow down onto the hard grassy shoulder.

The police car stops behind the carriage.

"Mr. Guardyall, you need a license to operate this on the road."

"Woof! Woof! Woof!" king barks and growls at the officer, who steps back.

"King, it's okay," Sam rubs his hand over the dog's nose. "Yes, I know. Sheriff Olsen informed me that I would. But I Just got this thing ready yesterday and thought, well, today would be a good day to see how it works. You know, Thanksgiving morning and all."

The officer writes him a ticket. "On Monday, get it taken care of. Now, turn around and take this back to your cabin and leave it there."

"But sir, I'm just a mile or so from my destination."

"I guess you did not hear me. I told you to turn around and take this unauthorized vehicle back to the cabin." He pauses. "I'll follow you to your road, with my lights flashing. So, turn this thingamajig around."

"Ah, dang it." Sam yanks the reins left, and Wonder pulls the carriage back on the road toward his cabin. Reaching his road, Sam waves at the police car as it continues with the lights off. In the barn, he unhooks the carriage and settles the horse in the stall, then fumbles for the truck keys so he can surprise Fran.

"Oh, my God. What is going on?" Sam grunts as he sees a flat tire on the drivers' side. A half-hour later, he drives out. Upon reaching the road to town, his cellphone vibrates and rings. He flips it open and sees the call is from Fran.

"Hello."

"Hey, Sam, I'm almost there, so don't go anywhere. You are home, aren't ya?"

"Yes, but almost not."

"Huh? What?"

"I'll tell you when you get here," Sam replies, and turns the truck around, and parks it in front of the barn. He runs into the cabin as King goes into the woods. He puts kindling and three logs on the fireplace embers when he hears the car stop at the porch. He goes to open the door.

"Fran, Happy Thanksgiving."

"Good morning, dear. How are you? Help me with all this," Fran says. "In the back seat are bags and a large oval pot."

"Is that a turkey in there?"

"Yes, it is."

"Full of surprises. What else? All the fixings too?" Sam carries the pot inside and sets it down on the butcher block table. Fran carries in two brown bags.

"There's one more in there," she tells him. Sam gets the last sack, and then holds his arms out for a hug and a kiss. Fran sighs and relaxes in his arms. "Happy Thanksgiving."

"You're making my day. When you called, I was on the way to surprise you. What all did you bring?"

"Oh, Sam, you won't believe it."

"What?" He cuts her off.

"This is going to be a Thanksgiving to go down in our history book. Meredith and Harry, and guess who else. Come on, guess."

"I thought Meredith was going to Harry's."

"Take a guess."

Sam hesitates, "Santa Claus?"

"Sam, I'll give you claws, right where it hurts. Counting us, it'll be eleven."

"Eleven? What? Who? Where'll we all sit?"

"Doctor Johansen is coming. Pastor Thomas and Mary, the sheriff, Marjorie, Paul, and Terri. So, we've got work to do. Meredith will be here soon to help."

"Wow. Ah …."

Fran cuts him off. "Meredith is bringing tables and chairs. And more food. Sam, you're just staring at me. What's wrong. I thought you'd be thrilled."

"Honey, the suddenness of it all. Give me a minute… an hour to comprehend it."

Fran grabs his hands, leans in, and softly her lips meet his. She whispers, "Go for a walk with King. Leave this to me."

"But..."

"No buts, go!"

Looking at her, at the table, the pot with the turkey inside, the stove, back to her, and his turkey in the icebox. He sighs. "All right. I'm outta here. It's all yours. Have fun."

Outside, King comes running. "Hey buddy, let's walk." They walk to the pier and then left into the woods. They reach the stream, where he reclines in the chair to look over the frozen lake and the snow-covered treetops.

Hmm? What a morning. Fran is preparing our Thanksgiving to beat them all. It's enough of a struggle for me to cook on that stove, and she thinks she can do it when she's never cooked anything here. Should I have given her grandma's notes before I left?. Am I second-guessing her abilities? She has watched me, but that's it. Well, it's still morning, and they will not get here for another, what, six-to-seven hours. How did she arrange for them all to agree to Thanksgiving in this cabin? Well, the sheriff is familiar with it, but the rest? The old doctor? Paul?.

"Lord, bless Fran and guide her. Keep her safe, and, yes, the cabin too." He reaches over to pet the dog. "You're cold." He starts the step-by-step slow walk along the stream up the incline and toward the road. He periodically stops to watch the waters roll over rocks. He pauses to look where the path rises away from two streams flowing together at a favorite spot to sit, meditate and watch the beavers work. *If those beavers keep it up, they will have a lake. Oh, there's one now.* "Hey buddy, I could use you to supply me with kindling for the fireplace."

King is sniffing tracts in the snow. Sam clicks his tongue. "Let's go." King leads his master up the path. They reach the road, turn left to follow the trail next to the road's shoulder, and follows King back to the cabin.

"Hmm?" Sam rounds the corner and stops. "Wow!" The memories of his first view seven months ago breeze across his mind. *That's all I could say when I first encountered this sight. I stopped and wondered if I had been transported back in time. And what did King do? He took off running and sniffing everything. This is one beautiful, fantastic view. Susan was right that this should be a National Geographic cover. Why don't I stop to take it in every time I come around this bend?*

"Oh well, that's life," he tells the air. Stepping on the porch, he opens the cabin door and sees Meredith fiddling with the cooking bracket in the fireplace.

"Meredith, you made it. No Harry?" Sam gives Meredith a welcome hug.

"Hi, Sam. He dropped me off but will be back in a few hours."

"Oh, honey, we need your help," Fran says.

"Ah, the queen needs the King's help," Sam replies.

"That's all you can come up with after an hour alone in the woods."

"Yep. Beaver John will be here shortly with more wood while the queen beaver prepares a turkey. Okay, what can I do?"

"First, we got two turkeys to cook," Fran says.

Sam replies, "What's the second item?"

Fran answers, "Second is for the king to tend to the queen's request. Diligently and promptly, like now without yacking."

Meredith chuckles, "Mom, I tried this King and Queen thing on Harry, and he looked at me as if I had lost my mind."

"Yeah, well, Sam may lose me if he continues with it."

"Okay," Sam says. "My grandmother wrote about fixing Thanksgiving turkeys for twenty-some friends. If she did it, so can we." He hands the note to Francinea and Meredith. "Read that while I set the fireplace up for roasting." He pushes the logs around to scatter the flames into embers. He sets up the metal brackets and rod. He adds some logs vertically to the rear and the sides of the fireplace to warm the bricks, plus two over the current embers. "Okay, we'll give them about twenty minutes to burn." Sam brings the rod to the table where Fran seasons the turkeys, and Meredith prepares the dressing. "When you're ready, push the rod through, and I'll hang it over the fire. It needs to be rotated every half-hour or so for five to six hours."

"Thanks, Fran says, wrapping her arm around his waist. " Your grandmother wrote that she followed the directions of your great-grandmother, with a few of her own embellishments. What would you have done without all the notes she left?"

"The original way of trial and error, I guess. Yeah, how did Eve prepare a Thanksgiving meal for Adam and the kids?"

"Sam, there's no mention of them celebrating Thanksgiving."

"Yeah, you're right. And that's been our ingrained problem ever since."

Meredith adds, "Our Thanksgiving holiday didn't start until President Lincoln declared in, what, 1863?"

"You get an "A" in history," Sam tells her. "Yep, once a year. One day, every year is set aside for thanks. So, for the rest of the year, there's no need to give thanks."

"Let's do that now," Fran says. The three of them hold hands as Fran expresses her gratitude for her many blessings. "For Meredith and Harry and their upcoming wedding on New Year's Day. For Sam and me too. And now, Father God, for this day, a special Thanks. Thank you, Lord."

"Amen," Sam says.

"Mom, thank you."

There's a knock on the door, and Harry enters. He hugs Meredith. "Not too late, am I?" he says as Fran's phone rings.

"It's Paul. Something came up at the grocery, and they won't be able to get here on time. Perhaps an hour late."

"Harry," Sam says. "Your job is to rotate the turkey about a slow quarter turn every half-hour."

"You're going to trust me to do that," Harry answers.

"Like the old days. Chores not done, no food."

Fran had informed everyone to arrive about three-thirty. It's now three. Sam monitored the oven temperature adding the right amount of wood when needed, and aided Fran and Meredith in preparing and cooking the side dishes.

"Looks like it's ready," Sam declares, removing the meat temperature gauge after cutting and tasting a slice of roasted turkey. Harry carefully carries the turkey to the table.

Meredith exclaims. "That's great," after chewing a chunk. "Oh, mom, I should have filmed all of this. It'd get many likes as a U-tube."

Sam asks, "No pies or bread?"

"The ladies offered to bring that," Fran answers. "They should be here."

Fran calls Doctor Johanson. "Huh?" She says after listening to him. "He won't be here. He's tied up at the Young Rascals Center." She carefully places the roasted turkey on top of steamed cabbage leaves as the centerpiece, and removes the stuffed dressing. She and Meredith empty the pots and pans of gravy, corn on the cob, beans, and steamed okra into bowls.

They put the two tables together along with eight chairs. All the food is covered with foil and ready to be served. A few seconds later, she tells Sam and Meredith, "Well, this is it. Thanks."

Sam gets a call from the sheriff, "he has had to fill-in for a deputy who called in sick."

Another knock, and Mary, carrying two pies, enter with Pastor Thomas, "Greetings." Happy Thanksgiving," he says. " Oh, that smells good. Thank You."

Mary hands the pies to Francinea and asks, "Where's Marjorie and the sheriff? We thought they were coming."

"Something came up," Fran says. "They won't make it, and neither will doctor Johanson. Paul and Terri may be an hour late."

"Oh, that's too bad," Mary says. "But then, in our experience, smaller group conversations are easier and more personal." She pauses and says, "Hey, you guys, we'll handle this. Go sit by the fireplace."

Comfortably on the couch, the pastor tells Sam, "We miss your grandparents. After Amilia passed on, Joshua had a tough time for a week or so. We spent many hours together, renewing his faith."

"I thought you had only been here six months," Sam states.

"You're right. Before I was appointed pastor here in Prairieville, I was the pastor of a church in Johnsonville. That's where we met your grandparents."

"Was that the church campus backing up to the golf course you pointed to?"

"Yes, that's it."

"Beautiful building. Why would you leave such an opportunity to teach the Word to so many as that offered? Oh, if I get personal, say so."

Pastor Thomas replies, "no problem. It was the elders. All they saw were numbers. They got excited at the growth and slowly demanded more and more leeway from me. They changed the respectful, quiet worship time that our generation grew up with to shout it out loud, bouncing music, if you call that music. They felt it would attract the younger generation. It did, and the church grew. When I heard about the opening here, I was led to apply."

As Harry rotates the turkey, he says, "are you saying that, well, the rock type music is, or cannot be God-worship-centered?"

"No, not at all." Pastor Thomas replies. "It has its place in society, just as the old hymns have their place. Our God, the creator of all, inspires all. It's what we as individuals personally do with it. The great commandment of our Lord demands love one another."

"Ah, the old hymns," Sam says. "Read the history of what inspired the writer to compose those, and you'll have a deeper feeling for them. Like Amazing Grace, by John Newton back in the eighteenth century. What a life …"

There's a knock on the door as Terri and Paul enter.

"We made it," Terri announces.

"Oh good," Fran says. "Now we can eat. Smelling and seeing this, I'm hungry. Pastor, would you say a blessing?"

"We're guests here, Sam, your home. It's your duty to say the blessing."

"Blessing," Sam says. "Okay, let's eat."

"Sam!" Fran scowls.

They all hold hands in a circle around the table. "Lord God, we thank you for all, yes, every blessing we have here today, and for yesterday too, and for the blessings we are not aware of yet. Lord, I could go on and on recalling all you've done for me, but not now. This is, well, you know, Thank You for this plentiful food. Amen. Oh, and thanks for the amazing hands of those who did it. Wow, the hand I'm holding now is so warm and so comforting, I don't want to let go. A thumb and four fingers, each of those having their unique imprint that identifies us. What these hands you created can do is beyond our comprehension." He feels a squeeze from Fran. "Okay, That's it. Thank You, Lord."

"Deep from your heart," Pastor Thomas says. "Now, let's eat."

During the conversations, Paul exclaims that he has been thinking of selling the store and retiring. Mary said she's exploring the possibilities of opening a girl's weekly meeting to address their expectation problems. The food was delicious and fulfilling.

Pastor Thomas suggests that Sam head up a men's weekly Bible study. "Sam, do it. I can help you pick a book to study. Also, how about a men's weekend retreat and worship time here at the cabin? Possibly do some fishing and have an archery contest. Sam, you've been put here for a reason. You've got a gift. Think and pray about it."

Eleven

"King, we've got company," Sam says as he sees the black car rounding the corner. He dons a jacket and cap, steps out on the porch to greet the man. "Welcome." Sam puts his hand in front of King's nose and says, "Sit!"

"Sorry, sir. But he's my Shepherd, and sometimes I'm his sheep to watch over."

"You are Mr. Samuel Guardyall, right?"

"Yes."

"Please sign here. This document indicates you have received notice that your right to this property will expire in three months.

"What?" Sam says.

"Yes. Here's the official document." He hands the envelope to Sam. "Please sign here. You do have the right to counsel provided by the court system or an attorney of your choosing."

"Are you telling me that I have to move in three months?"

"I am just the messenger. Thank you for your time," the man says and quickly drives away as King jumps and barks alongside the vehicle.

Standing on the porch watching the young man leave, Sam wonders: *Am I dreaming?* Sam opens the document and reads it.

He calls the sheriff. "Sheriff, I just got a visit from a guy from the Department of Interior. He said my right to this property expires in three months. He gave me an official-looking six-page document. This is goofy. What is going on?"

"Huh? Department of Interior?"

"Yes. And it has their stamp on the bottom."

Sam, I'll stop by this afternoon sometime," Sheriff Olsen replies.

"Okay, Lord, help me now. This cannot be."

Sam rubs King's neck. "Oh, buddy, I was hoping you would've jumped on him."

King moves his paw across the board and barks several times.

"Oh, you scratched the door. Good for you." Sam takes a long deep breath and sighs. "No. Lord, I'm sorry. Forgive me. I'm supposed to love my enemies."

He dresses for the cold, damp, windy weather. "We're going for a walk." He tells his pet lying on the porch. At his favorite spot, Sam stops, reclines in the chair, and peers into the distance over the frozen lake. He sees an eagle gliding near the shore, and suddenly it zooms in on a rabbit. *Wow! That rabbit just took off to avoid it. It knew the eagle was not a friend coming to say hi.*

Sam intently watches the eagle circling the area over the frozen lake, meeting the stream. "Wow! What eyes that bird has," Sam says, watching the bird a hundred feet or so above the stream dive down to get a fish. *Oh, now the fish, in a different realm, couldn't see the danger coming from the eagle's paws. The advantage goes to the eagle. Well, I guess we're somewhat like the fish. We're blind to the advancement of enemies while we go about doing our thing within our small realm. Those animals sense that danger is coming and do whatever they must to avoid it. Why can't we quickly recognize our enemies as the animal world does?*

"Lord, I didn't do anything against the native Indians. From the first in my lineage, my grandparents passed that deed to this acreage down to me. I need help, Lord."

Later that afternoon, the sheriff arrives. After reading through the papers, Sheriff Olsen tells Sam. "What they're implying is that Native Indians originally settled your acreage, and they claim they have the right to this land. It indicates that in 1856 your grandparents seized the land from the tribe, and now they want the land returned."

"My great-great-grandfather Ethan bought the land from some miner or farmer in 1864. I've got the deed to this land signed by the county supervisor. Isn't that enough?"

"Yes, Sam. To us, it is. But this is coming from higher up."

"Well, those in Washington ought to get off their butts and spend more time in the roots to see how reality works. I had some of the same problems dealing with them as I designed buildings. Some know-it-all behind a desk knew without looking that perhaps the foundation is not down far and wide enough. And then the cost of construction went up and up and up. They would always find something. That's their job, to find something that does not meet their standards they haven't informed us about. Yet. Yeah, that know-it-all got high-fives from the other know-it-all at the next desk. Oh, sorry, Sheriff, for my rant."

"I'm with you, Sam. Go see the county clerk. Search it out some more."

Sam swipes his tongue across his lips. "How about the National Forest? The tribe only occupied my little patch and none of the forest? Yeah, sure, that makes sense. It's only my ten acres they want? Back then, did the Indian tribe keep records like we do, and they have a written deed signed by the chief, or whoever?"

"Hey," the sheriff recalls. "Go ask Jason Whoduhaha. He may have some information about the tribes back then."

"Yes. Thanks. I'm not giving up without a fight, all the way to D.C. if I have to."

"See you again, Sam. That phone is working out for you, right?"

"Yes, it is Cousin sheriff. Thanks."

King and Sam sitting on the porch quietly watch the sheriff leave. "Shall we go for another stroll? Go see Fran? No. she's working. Yeah. Why not? Buddy, are you ready for a ride into town?"

"Woof."

On the way to Johnsonville, Sam thinks of what he intends to relate to Jason. He finds the old schoolhouse, knocks on the door, and pulls the handle. He knocks again and again louder. "Hmm? It's not quite four. The doctor said they have kids bunkered down here. Where are they? The staff? Supper time? Nap Time? Oh, if only I had Jason's number."

Sam opens his phone and calls Fran. Soon, a voice says, "Please leave a message."

"Hey, Fran. I'm at the old schoolhouse for the Young Rascals. It's all locked up, and I need to talk with Jason. Would you possibly have his phone number?"

Sam goes back to the truck to wait on a response from Fran.

What a name. Whodohaha. If my heritage was Native American, what kind of name would I have? Change Guardyall to Guarditall? Would that indicate that I was a warrior standing guard, watching over everything? Hmm? Whoduhaha must mean that he was, what? A comedian? Is that how the Indians got their names? Francinea could be Franseesneed indicating she's a doctor. The sheriff with the last name Olsen could be old son because he's the firstborn son. The native Americans have darker skin than we Europeans. How and when did we get split into different skin colors? They arrived in North America way back farther than Columbus in 1492. What sort of ship did they use to get here? With just canoes or fishing sailboats? No way could they have crossed the Atlantic from the Mediterranean area where it all started? When God destroyed that tower of Babel, he confused the common language and dispersed them. Did some of those families wake up the following day in Texas, Toronto, or Hawaii? Some in Brazil, Japan, Ireland, and Australia?

His phone rings. "Fran. Thanks for calling back."

"Honey dear," Fran says. "I'm so glad you got a phone. I'll be finished here in fifteen to twenty minutes. I'll meet you there. Okay?"

"Would you have Jason's phone number?"

"No, I don't. Call Doctor Johanson. He would know where Jason is. While at the restaurant, I put his number in your phone. Wait for me at that school, Sam. Don't go home."

"Thanks, I will. Love you."

Sam calls the doctor. "Doctor Johanson, I'm at an abandoned school, but it's all locked up. It's a block off Four-A, behind a seven-up station." Sam listens. "Okay, doc. Fran is on the way here."

"Let's walk around this school," Sam tells his dog.

As Sam walks on the sidewalk, King runs ahead and finds a tree beyond the empty playground. Sam stops to look in a window and the next two windows and through a door window. *Nobody here, and nothing inside. Is this the right vacant school where the ministry is locating?* He continues to walk around the school. As Sam is about to complete the walk, an older man hobbling with a cane makes his way to Sam.

"This property is off-limits. You can't be here."

"Woof, woof," King backs into a jumping position.

"King, stop it," Sam says, putting his hand in front of the dog's nose. "Sit!" Sam tells the stranger. "I thought this might be the building used by the Young Rascals."

"No, the rascals are down the road. A sign says so?"

"I saw the sign pointing this way."

"You need to leave," the man instructs.

"Sir, I'm Samuel Guardyall from Prairieville. I played in the Old Rascals golf outing this morning, where we heard about the ministry using an old school here in Johnsonville."

"I know anything about that. I call policc."

"You've got a bad leg, or is it your hip joint?" Sam asks.

"None of your business. Now, get going." He drops his cellphone onto the sidewalk.

Sam picks it up and hands it to him. "Here. What's your name? I'll pray with and for you."

The man makes a call. "I'm at school. A guy tried to steal my phone. Won't go. Got a big dog."

"I'll stay here with you and wait for the police," Sam tells the gentleman. "My dog is well trained and won't hurt you. Here, sit down on the bench." The old man sits with his arms on the cane as he stares into the distance.

Again, Sam says, "My name is Samuel Guardyall, and I live in a cabin near Prairieville."

"You're not Joshua?"

"No, I'm his grandson."

He looks at Sam. "Joshua! Let's go fishing."

"You knew Joshua?"

"A giant trout, and it broke my stick."

A lady dressed in white approaches. "Grampa, you shouldn't be here." She bends down to grab his arm, lifting him. "Here we go. We have some cake and ice cream ready for you. Sorry, sir," she tells Sam while holding the man's arm.

"How old is he?"

"He's ninety-two. Come on, Jax. Dessert time."

"I'm not Jack!" He hollers at the lady. "I'm going fishing with Joshua."

She rubs his shoulders and down his left arm, massages his neck, and down his back. "Jax, time to go home."

"Ma'am, my name is Samuel Guardyall. He seems to have known my grandfather, Joshua. I was looking for the Young Rascals Ministry school when he joined me."

"When you get to the main road, turn right, and it'll be right around the corner."

Sam holds their hands and prays, ending with, "Thank you. Lord, they're waiting to renew their strength. Amen."

"Can I help?" Sam asks.

"No need. We can do this. Thanks."

"Thank you, and blessings to you both."

Sam drives around the corner and into the lot of the ministry. He knocks a few times. He enters and walks the hallway looking for an office, when Dr. Johanson appears. "Hey, Doc."

"Samuel, I thank you so much for your contribution."

"Doc, Is Jason around. I need to speak with him."

"Jason? No, he's out getting supplies, and we probably won't see him till the morning. Let me show you around." The doc leads Sam from one room to another, describing the desires of the ministry. "In here is the inside play area where we'll have games and puzzles for the kids." He shows Sam the kitchen overlooking the cafeteria seating.

Sam hears shouts and screams coming from a nearby room. "What's that?"

"Ah, let's go see."

The doc opens the door to a classroom where they see hundreds of ballons being thrown in the air, at each other, ballons punched and broken. The kids are pushing and throwing many ballons at the twenty-something girl, who blocks them back at the kids.

Seeing the doctor and Sam, she blows a whistle three times. The boys and girls return to their desks, letting the balloons fall to the floor. "Very good," she tells the kids. "We have company. Now, all together say, "Welcome, Doctor Johanson.""

"Welcome, Doctor Johanson," the twelve children recite together.

"Well," the doctor addresses the kids. "this is Mister Guardyall. Say hi to him."

"Hi." One of the boys raises his hand.

"Yes, Patrick. What is it?"

"Is he here to guard us?"

Sam and the doctor chuckle as the teacher says, "Very good, Patrick. Class, give Pat a fist thump." The kids all hit their fists on the desks. "Someday, you may want to be a detective."

"Samuel, would you like to say something?" the doctor asks.

"Wow! I'm impressed. Do you know how lucky you are? God has brought you to this school for a very special reason. God saw you, each of you. He liked what he saw and made a way for you to come here. So, whenever you think about it, say thank you, God." Sam takes a breath. "I see that you've got a good teacher, and you won't need me to guard-you-all."

"Thank You, Martha," the doctor says. "Sam wants to see the rest of the school." Looking at the kids, he says, " Say goodbye to Mr. Guardyall."

"Goodbye. Bye-bye." They say.

In the hallway, Sam says, "Doc, I'm impressed. You've had these kids for how long? And you've been able to turn their lives around."

"It's been two months. Martha is the one. She's been the life and blood of ministering to them from the start, and she loves every moment. Some of them have started to call her mommy. Down the hall is what we're making into a gymnasium." He opens the door, and Sam sees one basketball hoop leaning against the wall. The floor is partially painted with stripes. "That's it so far."

"Sam," the doctor says. "We need more help to put all this together. Jason is great. He's contacted carpenters and plumbers to make major changes to the building during their time off, but we need others too."

"I'll be here tomorrow," Sam tells the doctor. "Doc, I was an architect before moving here. I'd love to help in any way I can, so look for me in the morning, about eight. Okay?"

"Thanks."

"Fran is on the way, so until then, lead me to the rooms Jason plans to renovate."

"You don't need me." He points toward the corner. "The second, third, and fourth rooms down that hallway. He's put markings on the floor."

"Thanks, I'll see you in the morning. Oh, doc. Would it be okay if I brought my dog?"

"Sure, the kids love dogs."

"He's a German Shepherd."

"So? Sam, I believe you would not have asked if you thought your dog would be harmful in any way. So yes."

Sam looks over each room, at the tape stuck to the floor, marking off the bedrooms for the kids, when Fran enters the room. "What's ya doing?" Fran asks.

"Hi, honey. Was just pondering how Jason plans to divide these into bedrooms."

She puts her arms around him and kisses his cheek. He holds her tight, then lifts and swings her around. "God is so good, Fran. He brought me beside the still waters and now leads me to go back to school to help in this ministry. Yes! And thanks to you, too. I've offered my services to make this one of the best children's ministries in the country. Look at what he's planned as bedrooms for the kids. Each of these taped areas will be for two kids. They'll enjoy the window, have a closet, and space for desks. Jason did this. Each classroom divided into three bedrooms. Twenty-one of them. Another classroom will be two big restrooms."

"I love it."

"And I love you more than ever. When you walked up on that stage, my heart pounded, and I knew then that God had something new in store for me. And this is it. I can't wait to get started."

"Sounds and looks great. I'm happy for you."

"Let's go celebrate with a good steak. Is Harry working this evening? How about Meredith?"

"The document you got? Have you heard anything more?"

"Wow! I forgot about that. Because of that fiasco, I came here to pick Jasons' mind about the Indian tribes. Tomorrow, I will. But, let's go. Oh, you gotta hear this. Doctor Johanson took me to a classroom where a teacher was having fun with twelve students. He introduced me to the students, and one of the boys raised his hand and asked if I was there to guard them all. Imagine that. A kid, oh, he was perhaps ten or eleven with that sense of perception. Honey, I can't wait to get started."

Twelve

"King, let's go. You're going to school today."

"Woof, Woof!"

After parking his pick-up, Sam and King enter the old school to find Jason. Approaching a classroom, he stops to peek through the door window and sees the teacher writing on the blackboard. Sam finds Jason in the first room around the corner.

"Jason, good morning," Sam greets him. "King, sit! I stopped by yesterday. Dr. Johanson toured me around the building, and I was able to see how you propose to divide these rooms. Looks good. I offered my services. Ready to help."

"And you are?"

"Samuel Guardyall. We briefly met at the country club banquet the other day."

" Yes. You're the one who got that cabin in the woods, right?"

"Yes, I inherited it from my grandfather."

"I wanted to ask you more about that, but we got interrupted."

"Yes, we did. If you don't mind, Jason, I need to talk with you about a threat I got from the Department of Interior. You got a minute?" Sam hands the pages to Jason. "Those ten acres of mine have been in the Guardyall name since the end of the nineteenth century. And now, suddenly, according to this, the government claim the right to repossess my ten acres."

"Samuel, I'm sorry. Yes, as you heard, I am of native ancestry. But what can I do?"

"Well, I thought that perhaps you might know the history of how the natives transferred properties. What records were kept, and by whom?"

Jason scans the document. "Samuel, right now, I can't help. Give me time, and I'll look into it. I've heard about some Native Americans pressuring the US to return their original land. I could be related to those back then, and I haven't been able to research that far back. Make a copy in the office for me, and when I get time, I'll work on it. But Sam, you can do it too. A google search."

"Can't. I don't have a computer."

"Oh yeah. No juice in the cabin. How do you manage that?"

"Considering each day as a vacation away from it all. Jason, right here and now, it's you and me. Millions of us live side by side in peace. And now, some knuckleheads want us to pay the price for what happened hundreds of years ago. Why can't we sit down together to peacefully talk this through? I've got a deed to that land." Samuel breathes deeply. "Lawyers! Politicians protecting themselves. Oh, sorry, Jason. But…"

"Sam, I'm sure you're aware of how your grandparents and those of that generation treated my ancestors. Give me time to see what I can find. I understand your position and how disturbing this must be, but right now, some contractors will be here shortly, and I'll be with them the rest of the day."

"Thanks. Now, what can I do to help divide these rooms?"

Jason looks at the dog. "First, tie him up on the playground. Sometime today, I'll use the office computer to check on this for you."

"Thanks, I would appreciate it."

"Take care of your dog, and then come help unload the materials. The truck should be here any minute."

Sam leads King outside and around the corner. "Woof! Woof!" King barks at seeing the children playing. King quickly jerks the leash out of Sam's hand and runs to where the children swing, slide, jump, and throw balls. King fetches a tennis ball, turns it over, and runs it back to the three little boys watching. Two kids turn and run away while one boy kneels, claps his hands, and whistles. King stops and drops the ball at the student's feet. The boy throws it. "Go get it," the boy hollers, and King trots after it.

The teacher approaches Samuel. "Sir, please! Please! Tie up your dog. He's scaring the kids."

"I'm sorry," Sam replies. "Jason told me to tie him up on the playground. I guess he wasn't aware the kids would be here."

"Oh, you're Mr. Guardyall. The doctor introduced you to the class yesterday."

"Yes, Martha," Sam says. "The boy now playing with King looks like the one who asked if I was here to guard them."

"Yes, that's Patrick."

"How old is he?"

"Patrick turned thirteen a month ago. He's a bright boy. Not afraid of anything. But, please, take your dog somewhere else."

"Yeah, but hey. I just had an idea if it meets your approval. Patrick seems to have already made a connection with King. Would you trust Patrick as the one to care for King while I'm inside working? He seems to have already made a connection with him."

Looking at the boy rubbing on King, Martha says, "Sure. I think he could do that."

"I'll check him out. How do the other kids treat Patrick?"

"Patrick," Martha, the teacher, says. "You remember Mr. Guardyall. That's his dog, and he'd like to ask you something."

"I'm just playing with it. I'm not going to hurt him," Patrick explains.

"I see that," Sam says. "His name is King. I see that King likes you, and you like King. Would you like to, ah, be in charge of and play with King today?"

"You're giving the dog to me? Hey," he yells at the other kids. "I got a dog. Oh, thank you."

"No, no, no," Martha says. "Mr. Guardyall is not giving his dog to you for keeps."

"What?" Patrick says as King returns with the ball. "When people give me something, it's for keeps." Patrick tries to get the ball out of King's jaws.

"You see that," Samuel tells him. "King has that ball but lets you throw it. So, this is like the ball. It's just for today."

"Yes, Mr. Guard-us-all. Where do I sign up to take care of King today? How about tomorrow? Oh, and thank you, Miss Martha."

Some of the other kids come to pet King. "Patrick," Sam says. "Show me what else you'd like to do with King."

Patrick looks down at King, enjoying the rubs from two students. "King!" Patrick says, bending over and looking the dog in the eyes. "Come!" Patrick runs to the soccer net. King is right alongside jumping and barking. The boy runs around the net, stops, and looks through the net at King on the other side. Patrick moves a bit to his left, stops, and leans right. King barks and runs after Patrick, who runs past the swings and climbs the slide ladder. He looks down at King, who has his front two paws on the third step. Patrick slides and throws the ball.

"Wow!" Sam says. "Martha, I've got food for King in the truck. He'll want some every couple hours."

"Patrick," Martha calls. "Now listen. The dog is your responsibility today."

"Yes, Miss Martha. I'll be good."

"That's what we expect. Go with Mister Guardyall to get some food for King."

On the way to the truck with the dog alongside, Sam questions Patrick. He tells Sam, "I never saw my father, and mom died when I was six. Then my brother Andy provided me food and a tent to live in while he worked. Then he got badly hurt in a wreck. Here I am."

"Thanks for sharing that with me. You're a smart kid; you know that? Here are some snacks and food for King." Sam reaches down to pet his dog. "King! Be good today." King and Patrick run back to the playground as Sam goes to find Jason.

"Okay, I'm back," he tells Jason in front of the computer. "Has the truck arrived?"

"No, they called and are having a problem. They'll be a couple of hours late. So, I'm searching this dilemma of yours."

While Jason searches online, Sam grabs a sheet of paper and begins sketching.

Ten minutes later, Jason tells Sam, " This is all I can find now. Some folks in a federal agency are working with the natives of tribes in several states. They are offering their services to rectify their wrong actions of long ago."

"That's it? How are the natives responding? There's got to be more specific details." Sam hands sheets of paper to Jason. "Here, while you were doing that, I made a few sketches for dividing the rest of the rooms."

"You just did this?"

"Yes. I was an architect. We designed homes, apartments, and hotels."

Jason answers his phone. "The trucks are here."

"Sam, I like it. Yes, I think Dr. Johanson would agree to use your plans for the girls, the restrooms, and the common area."

Jason and Sam help Bill and Robert unload the wood and supplies. They separate and stack them along the hallway. As Jason watches, Sam and the two carpenters start nailing the boards sixteen inches apart to form a ten by twenty-foot wall. Sam suddenly stops hammering. "Look at this." He says, holding the two by four in front of Jason.

"What?" Jason asks.

"The grain. Can you count the rings? Each of those lines supposedly represents a year of growth."

"So? Sam, put it in place, nail it. We're time-limited."

"How does it grow," Sam continues. "It's so hard. How does it transfer the nutrients from the soil through this hardwood to a branch fifty feet up, enabling leaves to grow? Look!" Sam pours a few drops of water on the wood. "See! Some of the water rolls off. The wood absorbs some, but is that it? So, how does a tree grow so tall and straight? And to think it started as a seed like that bristly cone."

"Sam! It's a two-by-four. Put a nail in and see if it screams."

"Screams? Oh, did the tree scream when it was cut down? That tree was full of life, and now we're nailing it. If you cut my leg off, I'd scream."

"Sam!" Jason yells and yanks the two-by-four from Sam. He places it on the floorboard, swings the hammer at a nail, and hits his thumb. "Yoweeeee!"

Sam peers at Jason, holding his red thumb. "Oooh, that had to hurt. Go put some ice on it. We'll finish this. Go!"

The three guys set it upright, making sure it's vertically straight, and nail it to the outside wall, the floor, and the ceiling. An hour later, Jason returns with his bandaged thumb. "Martha did it." He says.

"She's a beauty," Sam winks at Jason. "Did you notice my dog anywhere?"

"He was lying on the floor next to Patrick. Wow! You did all this while I was gone? Thanks, your help is much appreciated. As you've no doubt seen, my studies have been theological, not carpentry."

"Oh," chuckling, Sam replies, "But you know how to hammer."

"Yeah, right. You three can handle the rest. I'm taking a break."

"A break? Ah, the thumb is hurting again? Want to see Martha, huh?"

Sam, Bill, and Robert finish dividing two more rooms.

"What's in store for tomorrow?" Sam asks.

"We'll be hanging the drywall sheets and rolls of insulation," Bill says. "Be ready about ten." He pauses and steps close to Sam and speaks softly. "Sam, your grandfather reviewed history in one of my high school classes. He made it more interesting by concentrating on the average person's experience throughout history, rather than the federal version of famous names and dates."

"When was that?"

"Eight years ago. I graduated the next year."

"Grandpa was eighty-three then. How about you, Robert?"

"No, I'm from Denver. My wife was from here, so we moved here after our marriage two years ago."

"Was she going to school in Denver?"

"Yes, we met at a church picnic."

"Well, guys. I need to get my dog and head home. I've enjoyed working with you guys, But, hey, tomorrow, take it easier on this old dude."

"Ten o'clock," Bill says.

Sam walks down the hallway, peeks into the office, and then the classroom. When he steps inside the room, King barks and runs toward Sam, and then turns and runs back and licks up the treat Patrick held.

Patrick says, "See that! He chooses me as his owner."

Martha says, "Now, Patrick...."

"What?" Patrick interrupts. "He gave me the dog. It's mine."

"King!" Sam kneels and claps his hands. "Come!"

"Patrick, let go of the leash," Martha instructs.

"No! It's my dog." Patrick exclaims, and the rest of the kids start thumping their fists on their desks, shouting, "Yes. Yes. Yes."

"Stop that. Now!" Martha yells and blows her whistle, but the kids keep pounding.

"Mister Guardyall?" She softly says, looking to him for help.

"Stop it!" Sam tells the kids as he goes to get King. "Sorry, Patrick. But it's time for King to go home. If I bring King back tomorrow, do you promise that you'll let King go? No fits. No disturbances. Otherwise, King will stay home while I'm here, and you won't get to play with him again. Do you promise?"

Patrick pounds his fist on the desktop. "King likes me. I like him."

"I know that, but it's time for King to go home with me."

"Miss Martha, why can't we get one to keep?" Patrick asks.

"King is not always fun," Sam tells the students. "Sometimes he goes too far, like the time when he got sprayed by a skunk. Wow, did he stink, and I did too when he came for a hug and rub. He had to be cleaned by a professional, and I had to clean that smelly, yucky stuff off my clothes. Another time he got hit by a car, and I had to carry him into the vet's office, and he's heavy. Then he had to wear a brace on his leg. Are you ready for things like that?"

"Class, having a dog to rub and chase the ball is more than just fun," Martha adds. "Class, I'm stepping out a minute to talk with Mr. Guardyall."

She closes the door.

"I'm sorry, Martha," Sam says. "It might be better if I did leave him in the barn."

"Yes, please do. I'll check with the doctor about possibly getting them a dog. But a smaller one. Oh, this gives me an idea for a class project."

Sam and King leave the school, and at the hospital, he checks the parking lot for Fran's car. Not seeing it, he drives home. King runs to the barn.

After warming the cabin and fixing his coffee, he calls Fran. "Hey, how ya doing?" Sam asks.

"Hi, honey. Glad you called. I thought you would stop by the hospital before you went home."

"I did. I drove around the lot looking for your car."

"Meredith dropped me off this morning. Sorry. Sam, we only have two weeks to New Year and my new life. And Christmas is around the corner. No gifts Sam. There's a lot we must do. Come back to the hospital to get me. I'll be finished here in an hour, and then we'll go to the cabin."

"Sure. I'll have a few minutes to stop and check with Jason. Bye."

Sam stops at the school and finds Jason and Doctor Johanson still in the office.

"Sam," Jason says. "Got some more information for you. It's the Department of Energy that's working with the Wyoming Tribal Settlement. The department wants that land and is willing to trade the Northern Forest for the barren tribal land there in Wyoming."

"Huh? Why?"

"Ah. So far, all I can discover is that it's a sort of retribution by the government. That's what they say. Someone by the name of Outmore is negotiating."

Sam interrupts, "Outmore, you said?"

"Yes, a Frank Outmore. He's been negotiating for the department with the tribe."

"He was with the Fish and Wildlife Agency when he told me I couldn't connect to the grid to update the cabin. What's he got to do with this?"

"According to what I saw on the web, he's offering them the federal land surrounding the lake, which includes your cabin. Got something to do with the feds wanting the land they now occupy. They say it's better than an even trade. He tells them they will get a cabin for ceremonies, the forest for hunting, and the lake for fishing. The area they now occupy is barren and dry."

"Where is that?"

"About a hundred miles northwest across the border in Wyoming."

"That's it," Sam says.

"What?"

"Oh, nothing. Jason, I may be late tomorrow. Would you copy those web addresses for me?"

Jason copies them and pastes them onto a Word document and prints it for Sam.

"Thanks. You're a blessing. Oh, at times like this, I need my computer."

"Get one and extra batteries."

"Anyway, thanks again, Jason. Now I've got to get my fiance'. You might see me tomorrow. I don't know how, but I've got to get this settled soon. Pray with me."

Jason and Sam hold hands and kneel. Jason asks the Lord to lead, guide, and sanctify Sam in this problem distressing him. "And for all those involved, clear the confusion and let it be peaceful for all."

"Thanks. I must get more clarity on this soon." Sam leaves to get Fran at the hospital. He finds her on a bench outside the emergency door.

"Sam, it's so good to see you. I missed you," Fran says as she gets in the truck.

"I missed you too, but oh, this thing about the cabin is causing dizziness."

"Let me see," Fran says as she feels his forehead and looks deep into his eyes.

"No, I don't feel physically dizzy. It's the run around trying to get a handle on that idiotic declaration."

"What can I do?" Fran asks as she holds his hand.

"Nothing. Just pray that this goes away. Would you mind if we got take-out and go rest in the cabin?"

"Sure. Arby's is on the way."

They use the drive-thru and head to the cabin, where King greets the truck. "Hey, boy!" Sam pets the dogs' head and rubs behind the ears. Relaxed on the couch by the fireplace, they eat the sandwiches and fries while Sam updates Fan on the events of the day. "Jason discovered that the guy who told me I couldn't change anything but then offered wind or solar is the one involved in this."

"He was with the Fish and Wildlife Agency, right?" Fran says. "What does that agency have to do with Native Americans and where they live?"

"Got me. In the morning, I'm going to the county courthouse to check the records of my ten acres. Colorado became a state in 1876, so there may be records going back to 1900. This whole thing is driving me up the wall."

Fran folds the quilt blanket and lays it on her lap. "Honey," Fran says. "Here, lie down, close your eyes and let me rub behind your ears."

"Rub my ears?"

"Sure. Why not? It works for King." Fran smiles, leans over to kiss her husband-to-be. "Tomorrow, while you're checking on that, I'll be sending out the invitations. It's just a couple of weeks away. Are you ready for that change?"

"Are you ready? Ready for a name change from Outmoure to … Egads. That guy's name…! Sorry!"

"That's okay, hon. You need a good, quiet, peaceful rest."

She lowers his head and shoulders down onto her warm blanket-covered lap. He relaxes, gives in, and then closes his eyes. "You're sweet." He mumbles.

"Sweeter than the barbeque sauce?" Fran softly says as she starts rubbing Sam's neck down his arm and massages his neck tendons. She softly sings, "Now I lay me down to sleep…."

Thirteen

"Oh my," Francinea says. "Sam, wake up! It's eight-forty," as she pushes against his shoulder.

"What?" Sam asks.

"Yes! We had a two-hour nap. I've got to get home!"

Standing and stretching, Sam looks at Fran, tossing the blanket over the couch. "Ah, that felt good. Thanks."

"Take me home," Fran tells him. "I got a day in the office tomorrow." She calls Meredith. "Sorry Mer, I'm at Sam's, and I just woke up from a nap." She listens to her daughter and then exclaims, "No, we did not. I fell asleep on the couch. Sam will drive me home. Have you done that book report?"

Sam and Fran, with King riding in the trucks' bed, head to Fran's. On the way, Sam updated her on what Jason found on the web. He also detailed how Patrick enjoyed playing with King. "Could I use your computer for a bit?" Sam asked her.

"Sure, after I check my scheduled appointments for tomorrow." Arriving at the house, Fran knocks on Meredith's door. "I'm here."

"Yeah, mom, gimme a second," Meredith says with a raised voice. Fran returns to the kitchen, opens her laptop, and checks the schedule.

"Hey, Sam." Meredith greets him as she enters the living room. "Took a nap, eh?"

"Yeah. Your mother was petting behind my ears. I relaxed and, well, that was it. So how's it going with school? Are you getting passing grades? Hmm? Well, here comes Harry." He strolls into the living room from Merediths' bedroom, as she goes into the kitchen.

"Samuel, are you ready for the big day?" Harry asks as he sits near Sam on the couch.

"How about you? Are you ready? I've done this before, but you haven't."

"We've been discussing it. It's a first in the state and most states. The principal finally okayed it but laid down some rules we must follow."

"Rules? Like what?" Sam asks.

"We can't hold hands. If in the same class, we must be seated on opposite sides of the room. And, we must maintain the same grades that we had before. We must treat the other students the same as we did before. We cannot talk about the wedding, nor anything else connected with it during school hours. And…"

Sam cuts him off. "How will they monitor that?"

"He's giving us bracelets to wear on our wrists at all times within school properties."

"Bracelets? How's that gonna work when you're practicing or playing a game? Oh," Sam corrects his thinking. "The football season will be over."

"We've got one game Friday, and that's it if we lose. If we win, then more."

"Your record is great so far. Seven and one. Who do you play Friday?"

"Johnsonville Bears."

"Another one with them? How do you feel about your chances this time?"

"Much better. The coaches have been studying them since we got whipped the first game. We gotta win this one. Our last chance to make the finals?"

"Good luck. I'll be there to cheer you on."

"You should cheer us on in the locker room before the game. Your positive chats encouraged me to keep at it. So, how about it?"

"Nah! that's the coach's job."

Harry asks, "Mery briefed me about the letter you got. How's that working out?"'

"So far, it's been a nightmare. Imagine the backlash …"

Fran, peeking into the living room, says, "Sam, you can use the computer," "Oh, hi Harry. I didn't hear you come in."

Sam goes into the kitchen, sits at the dining room table, and starts his search. Fran gives Harry a hug. "You ready for the big game tomorrow?" She asks. "Mer, you're just standing there. Are you not welcoming Harry?"

Meredith gives Harry a hug and a kiss.

"We need to discuss our plans. Have you mentioned anything?" Harry asks her.

"I haven't had time." She looks her mother in the eyes. "We've been thinking of postponing our wedding until after graduation."

"Huh? Why would you do that?"

"The principal did okay it, but under certain conditions. We cannot publicize it in any way, along with other things. That stupid bracelet we must wear. But now the other students are scared they may have to wear one, and they're blaming us. I'm losing friends."

"Oh, I'm sorry. But the principal, did he address the school? The school board? What have they said?"

"They're leaving it up to the principal. But I think he is scared of losing his job if he fully supports us, or someone resists and spreads rumors."

Sam listened to them as he was clicking icons on the computer. He adds, "The pressure must be coming from the state. That's how it works. They turn it over to the next level down, the next level under them, and on and on. If it doesn't work to their advantage, the blame goes to the incompetence at the lowest level."

"Meredith, honey, are you okay with that then? Originally, we all thought it'd be great to have a mom and daughter wedding at the same time. Sam, How about us? I don't want to, but would it be okay with you to postpone our wedding?"

"No. No way! The word is out, and I know Sheriff Olsen and Marjorie canceled their vacation plans to be here. And didn't your supervisor at the hospital say something like that?"

"Yes, she did."

"Well?"

"Yes. okay," Francinea says. "Ours on New Year Day, and Meredith and Harry sometime after graduation. Hmm? Yes, Mer, the waiting time adds more to its excitement. You'll be glad you did."

"Okay." Meredith then says and gets a thumbs up from Harry.

"So, first thing at school tomorrow, you two go tell the principal."

Sam closes the laptop, stands, and says, "Hon, I should go. It's getting late."

He does. Driving through the town square, he sees the sheriff's van parked in front of the diner but continues home.

After firing up the fireplace and the stove, and a fresh cup of coffee in his hand, he lights the lantern at the desk. "Now, King, I need to do this now, so sit!"

My Cabin Life 21

Ah, time is moving faster than ever. Well, it seems that way. And with it, the demands, the expectations, the desires, the opportunities all seem to collide. Like our initial plan of a mom and daughter wedding flew out the window because it's not one of those previously accepted societal norms we live under. How do they get formed, get accepted, and followed by everyone?

Go back in history, and kids were getting married when they reached puberty. Now, since the implementation of the public school system, when was that? A hundred, two hundred years ago? Now it's not acceptable for senior high school kids, several years through puberty, to be married before graduation. Ah, would they cheat on homework assignments discussing the details together as they relax on the double bed?

Questions.

Yes, the computer and the internet escape me now. No, I escaped that. Yep, I could have pressed a few buttons, scrolled, and would have the answer right here in black and white and possibly a colored picture too. At times like this, I yearn for it. The ten minutes this evening on Fran's laptop, I did discover some of the why and who originated the plan to kick me out. That Outmoure guy. He did not like it when I declined his offer of a wind turbine or solar panels, implying that the agency would pay for it. He'd do that but did not want me to connect to the grid. Why?

If this comes to pass, and the tribe takes over, will Frank inspect every deer that is shot? Will the agencies watch and see if the tribes make adjustments to the cabin? Will they now allow motorized boats on the lake? For water skiing, for races, or just an enjoyable afternoon fishing? Will they also give the forest north of the road to the tribes? Will the tribe keep the cabin as it always has been?

Well, anyway, a new day in the morning, the Lord willing. And if no new day comes, I won't care one inch.

Now Tomorrow.

One. To the county courthouse for the history of my deed.

Two. Back to the little rascal schoolhouse.

Three. An enjoyable evening with Fran.

Sam is warmly dressed, has the documents, has his copy of the deed, and with King on the passenger seat, he heads to the courthouse. He is directed to a different office, then another, and asked to wait. He finally sees his number posted. He's asked to provide his name, address, driver's license, and a copy of a utility bill. "Ma'am, It's a log cabin. I'm not connected to anything. No water, no sewer, no electricity. I get my water from a well, and the waste goes back to nature."

"Okay, have a seat, please."

Soon, a heavy-set gentleman opens a door.

"Mr. Guardyall, come on in. I've looked at your records, and everything is up to date. Your grandfather made sure it was according to all our records going back to 1901. So, relax and throw this in the trash." He points to it, and hands the document to Sam. "This is a hoax. Someone is trying to defraud you. We've been unable to verify who is doing this, but they will be arrested when and if. These things are happening more and more through the internet."

"But the stamp," Sam says. "It looks like the real thing. And the pages I've seen on the net even named the agency and the fellow responsible for overseeing it. How can those numerous articles be fake?"

"Yes, I know what you're saying, but that's the way things are in this world of fake news. The document itself is just MS Word, done in ten minutes. The stamp is copied and replicated. I suppose they leaked something on the net, and a news agency picked it up, and they had the headline of the week. And on and on it goes. So, Mr. Guardyall, you're safe in that cabin. No one can force you out, not us, the state, or the feds. And Sheriff Olsen will be there for you.

"Are you sure of this? I don't want a mob or whatever suddenly appearing to take over my cabin."

"Yes! Positively. Absolutely. I'm sure of it. This kind of stuff is happening more and more. Lots more in the cities and suburbs, In rural communities like this, we get to know our neighbors more so than in the big cities. A small county court manager like myself goes to church with the residents. You're safe here." He pauses. "And, by the way, I'd like to thank you for ministering to my son, Harold. He was at a weekend scout camp you had."

"Harold? Ah, yes, I remember him. He's a smart kid And brave too. How's he doing?"

"Wonderful. He's working out like crazy. Push ups. Lifting weights. Running. Every week, he asks me to measure his triceps and biceps and his waist. He wants to play football. He looked at me one evening not long after that weekend and asked: "Dad, how come you're so fat? Gads, I wanted to punch him. So, Mr. Guardyall, it's been my pleasure to meet you finally. And don't worry about that letter. It's bogus." He breathes deeply. "When you plan another scout campout, I'd like to be there."

"Mr. Stevenson, Gene, and I have talked about it, but winter is here, so it'd probably be sometime in the spring. When that time comes, I'll make sure Gene puts you on the list. Thank you. Thank you so much for being so honest. What you've said about this is just another sign of this computer-driven age. Nothing is off-limits or secret. I'm getting married on New Years Day, so you're welcome to come."

"Thank you, Mr. Guardyall."

"Call me Sam, and I'll let Fran know to send an invitation, and please bring Harold too. No gifts! please."

Sam leaves the courthouse, jumping and shouting. "Hallelujah."

Back in the truck, Sam heads to the schoolhouse.

Sam is about to park the truck when he remembers he agreed to leave King in the barn for the day. He was about to turn around and go home, when Patrick comes running toward him with Martha following.

"King! King!" Patrick yells.

Martha waves at the truck. Sam breaks. "Oh, I'm in trouble now," he mumbles. Arriving at his window, Martha says, "Sam, it's alright. Doctor Johanson agreed to allow Patrick another day or so to watch over your dog."

"You're sure it's okay?"

"Yes. Pat and I talked it over, and he understands. No fits. Nothing but playing with King. He understands it's temporary fun."

Sam opens the door for King, who gets petted and rubbed. He parks the truck, gets out, and watches Martha, Patrick, and King run to the playground as he enters the building. He finds Jason, Bill, and Robert partitioning the second room.

"Hey, Sam. Glad you could make it," Jason greets him. "We finished the drywall of the first room. So grab a hammer."

"How's that thumb?"

"Much better."

The four of them get the second room walled off, the third room, and then Lunch and conversations. Sam starts talking to Jason. "That document I showed you is fake."

"Huh? Fake? No, it couldn't be."

Sam relates what he learned at the county courthouse.

"But Sam, From what I've read, the tribe is expecting it. They've accepted the plan."

"But that's fake too. I got an idea on the way here this morning. To be sure, how about if we drive up there and discuss it with them. Would they be agreeable to a visit?"

"They've made it into a tourist site. Everyone's welcome, but to sit down and talk with the chief, I dunno."

"Let's try it anyway."

"But, I can't go until the week or so after New Year."

"That'll be fine, the last of January."

The rest of the afternoon, they finish the drywall on the two rooms.

"Guys, I can help a couple more days, then it's Christmas, and New Year is fast approaching. Then I'll be tied up for the ceremony preparations," Sam says.

He gets King, and heads home to wait on Fran. He calls the sheriff after warming the cabin and having a pot of coffee ready. "Hey cuz, that document I got declaring I had three months left in the cabin, and then the Navajos would take over. It's a bunch of baloney. One of those scams."

"I know, Sam. Just minutes ago, I finally got to talk with Frank Outmore. He's been out of the country and not taking calls. We talked for a few minutes, and then I texted him the picture I took of the document. After looking at it, he burst out laughing. Yeah. He said of all the people he's dealt with, he never would have suspected that you'd be one to fall for that."

Silence.

"Sam, are you still there?"

"Yes, I'm here." Sam softly replies and hangs up. He leaves a note for Fran. He dresses warmly, puts on his boots, gets the flashlight, takes King to the barn, and goes out for a walk. He walks along the snowy path to his favorite spot by the stream.

Fourteen

Arriving at the cabin, Fran reads the note pinned to the butcher block table. "Huh?" She removes her nurse shoes and pulls on the boots. She is warmly dressed and follows Sam's snowy footprints to the stream, finding Sam leaned back in the camp chair.

"Sam, honey, are you all right?" Fran asks as she rubs his shoulder.

"Oh, hi. You startled me."

"Are you okay?"

"I don't know. How could I?"

"How could you what?"

"How could I fall for it, like I did? Let myself get upset and everyone else too over a piece of paper. That's all I've been thinking about the last few days, and here it was, just a dumb scam. And I fell for it. How could I? Why?"

"Huh? Fell for what?"

"A simple scam that any fifth grader would have seen right away. And I was so concentrated on that threat of losing my cabin and my relationship with everyone. It consumed me for days. What a jerk."

"What? This is about that letter? Did you say it was a scam? A fake? And you're upset? You should be overflowing with joy."

"I fell under its spell, and I was bringing everyone else into it too: the sheriff, Gene, you, Jason, the doctor. I forced them to stop what they were doing to listen to me, a bum. Yeah, a bum living on the street would have immediately tossed it in the fire. But not me."

"Sam, my dear," Fran holds his hand. "You know what. One of the reasons why I love you so much is that, yes, you love God, but you are human too. You try your best, but then that human nature outwits, as it does to all of us. You've wanted to appear how much closer to God you are because, well, you, Samuel Guardyall, live in a log cabin without what the rest of us enjoy."

Sam turns his head and looks her in the eyes.

Fran pulls on his forearm. "Get up, and let's go inside where it's warm, and have a drink."

He struggles to stand. After a few steps supported by Fran, he straightens, sighs, leans his head toward Fran, "Thank you." His arm goes around her in a tight hug. "Oh, I love you. But how could you love me after all my ranting over nothing?"

"Why? Because you're human, just like me. So, let's get down to basics, and I'll take you as my husband this evening."

Sam stops, looks her in the eyes, and chuckles. She bursts out laughing. He grabs her elbow, forcing her to fall to the ground. He lies there next to her in the snow. They quietly gaze at the clear star-lit sky.

"So many of them," Sam says. "Thousands? Millions? Oh, there goes one. How dark and clear it is. It's like looking into nothing but everything. Oh, Lord, it's marvelous. And you put them out there for us."

"Beautiful."

Raising his voice, he hollers, "Hello, up there! Hello!"

A few seconds later, he says, "Did you hear that?"

"What? I didn't hear anything."

"Yes," he points to his forehead. "I heard it clear and sharp. Come to me, all you who are weary, and I will give you rest."

"Oh! What timing," says Fran.

They relax a bit in quiet wonder, and then Fran pushes a fist of snow into his face and rolls away.

"Oh, you're going to get it," Sam says. He crumbles some snow and tosses it at her.

She blocks it and starts running toward the cabin.

He catches up to her, lifts her off her feet, and carries Fran into the cabin, where he sets her down on his bed. He looks down at her. "You've got two minutes."

"Two minutes? Oh, you're going through with it. Yes, I want to hear your vows. On your knees. Now!"

"You've got two minutes to fix me some coffee. I'm going to the barn to get King."

"What?" Fran yells, "Chicken!" He opens the door and steps onto the porch. She removes her coat, knee-high boots, gloves, strikes a match to the kindling in the stove, and starts pumping water into the pot. She measures the coffee grounds into the basket and sets the coffee pot on the lighted Coleman stove. At the fireplace, she ignites new kindling and three logs. Looking at her watch, she mumbles, "Where is he?" Returning to the kitchen area, she adds wood to the stove. The door opens, King barks and runs to her for a rub. Sam notices the fireplace glowing, feels the warmth coming off the stovepipes, and sees the pot brewing coffee.

Alongside her at the butcher block table, Sam gets on his knees. Looking up at her, he starts, "Francinea Ingersoll, I love you. I'm going to ask you again. Will you become my wife forever and ever?"

"Yes! And I agree again," and they passionately kiss, rocking back and forth.

"Oh, Fran. You rescued me this evening. I owe you so much. It's too late to go get a good steak, but what can I do for you?"

"You already did it. Now go sit down. I'm calling for delivery."

"Twenty minutes." She says, joining Sam on the couch by the fireplace. "To bring you up to date, I mailed thirty-two invitations yesterday. And there are more inquiries every day. How are we going to do it? We can't get over one hundred here in the cabin."

"Okay. How about this? Do it like they must have done in pre-biblical days. No pastors or priests. The parents gave their kids the freedom to leave to join another and start having children. A father presented his daughter to the son of a neighbor's family. They said the vows, danced, and had a merry ole time with a feast, and that was it. Hmm? Do we need pastors? We will say the vows, dance, and sing, and send everyone home."

"Sam, come on, this is serious. The invitations indicated it'd be here. Now, we've got to figure out how to do it."

"Hmm? Let's have two," Sam says. "One at ten in the morning and the second at four or five that afternoon. Or, as you suggested, call the ceremonies off and consummate it here tonight." He chuckles.

"You'd like that, wouldn't you?"

"It was your idea," Sam responds and gets a slap on his forearm.

"Think about that double you suggested," Fran says. "Yuck, it'd also require double preparations, double everything. No, forget that. Nice idea, but."

"Here's another. In front of the gazebo. We put up a tent, rent a bunch of chairs."

"No! it'd be too cold."

"Portable gas heaters!" Sam replies.

There's a knock on the door.

"Ah, just in time," Fran says, and in walks Harry and Meredith, carrying two sacks.

Harry announces, "We've got your favorite, Sam. From the Johnsonville butchery."

"Mom, you wouldn't believe what happened today. But first, come and get it."

Sam opens one of the styrofoam containers and sees a one-inch thick beef steak. "Oh, thanks, Harry. My belly was itching for one of those. And those rings of fried mushrooms. Thank you. You two are a blessing."

He shakes Harry's hand and hugs Meredith.

Fran opens the box to see her favorite roasted steak with a stuffed baked potato. Looking at her daughter, Fran says, "What happened? Are you okay?"

"Oh, yes. I got an A-plus plus on my book report. The teacher told me I've got a gift to write. Said I should be a journalist."

"Huh? A journalist?"

"Eat, mom, and we'll talk about this later."

Sam blesses the food, Meredith and Harry. He adds: "Lord, this ceremony of marriage coming. Guide us, lead us. It's become a riddle. So many obstacles. Please, Lord, provide the way, help us with those decisions. Amen, That's it. Now let us enjoy this food for our bodies."

"Harry, you're not working tonight?" Sam asks.

"I have already. My four hours, six to ten."

"Oh, yes. Time flies when having fun. The steak is great. Thanks."

"As we were about to leave, Meredith got the call. I was able to get the dinners, and here we are." He reaches for Merediths' hand, "Let them eat." As they take the first steps toward the fireplace couch, Harry turns to Sam and says, "You could leave a tip."

After finishing the food, Sam and Fran join Harry and Meredith.

"Now, Meredith, tell me more of this journalist thing," Fran asks, after settling down next to her daughter on the couch as Sam reclines in the cushioned chair.

"I enjoy writing. Have been for some time now. When she told me that, it hit a nerve, and I'm beginning to think more about a writing career."

"This is a surprise. You've been helping animals with the vet to get a start. What about that? The nursing career?"

"I can do that too. I've started writing about the insides of the medical field, what nurses and doctors do to comply with their vow to do no harm. My teacher loved the idea. I'll show you what I've written so far when we get home."

"Harry," Fran asks. "what do you think of this?"

"I've seen some of her writing, and it's good. It kept me interested to read more. If that's what she wants, then good. She should go for it."

"Oh, Mer, I guess I'm just shocked after all those years you've been single-minded on helping people. But, if that's what you really want, then yes."

"Sam," Harry says. "How's your investigation going? Discover any more details?"

Fran quickly answers. "It's all over. Done. He won't have to move."

"How?" Harry asks.

"The county mayor took care of it," Sam says. "Harry, have you experienced a scam or hoax on that computer of yours?"

"Every day. But I got a software program that blocks it."

"But, if someone showed up at the house and presented an official-looking document telling you that the Denver Broncos had canceled your scholarship, what would you do?"

"I guess I'd make a call. First, the U. of Nebraska, and if I had to, I'd call the Broncos."

"Meredith, you're a lucky gal to have found Harry. And I'm very fortunate to have Fran by my side." Sam takes a deep breath, looks down a moment, and then at each of them. "I got a confession to make. This evening, I doubted myself and what I'm doing here. A depression set in. I was upset with, well, with me. I had to get away, so I went to my favorite spot to un-think. Oh, those thoughts were like an Olympic competition in the four hundred meter free swim that had no end. They were bouncing around my head and running into each other, causing more confusion, more doubts. And all of that just because I let myself down. I believed a lie. Bewitched, or as Fan called it, I let myself be out-witted. Yeah, me, who has it all together, didn't see through the maze of an easily opened hoax, and I needed help. Me, ask for help? I knew Fran would be stopping here on her way home, so I left her a note telling her I needed to be alone this evening. She came anyway. After a few moments of listening to me moan, she saw me as I am, and I didn't like that either. Then, she made an offer, one that would certainly be pleasurable. That little bit broke my doubts wide open, and I started laughing. Yeah, laughing at me." He pauses. "Oh, God is so good. All the time. Knew what I needed at that time, so He sent Fran to rescue me."

"Remember this," Fran says. "This may be the last time Sam comes down to our human level."

"I'll show you right now what a real human can do when irked," Sam says.

"Go ahead. Oh, should Mer and Harry leave first?"

"Nah, they're amateurs and may need to see how's it done. Harry, watch."

"Mom, Sam. Stop it." Meredith exclaims.

"Oh, no. This is interesting," Harry says.

"Sorry, Mer," Fran says. "Okay, Sam, hon, you won that one."

"Yahoo!" Sam replies. "I won!"

Fran tells Meredith. "We've made a decision. Our wedding ceremony will be right here in a tent by the gazebo using portable gas heaters. "You will chauffer me in Sam's horse-drawn carriage."

"Yes. I love it. YES!"

"It's settled then. Sam, honey, you've got some work to do."

"Don't I always. We agree, and that's it then. Ten days to go. Now, Fran, what's on your agenda for tomorrow?"

"Sunday. Church, of course. Come over to the house about ten, and we'll go together. Aren't you scheduled for a talk?"

"Oh, wow!" Sam replies. "I almost forgot. I've got some reading to do. Thanks. Ten you said? It's been quite an evening. Thanks. Fran, you helped me to put the armor back on. And

Meredith, you're always a delight to see. Now you take care of Harry and help him get his grades up to your level."

Harry says, "That was just for a book report. That's all. Sam, perhaps, you ought to start writing your thoughts into a journal."

"He has and is," Fran says. "Well, It's late, and we need to go. Good night." She hugs and kisses Sam and steps onto the porch with Harry and Meredith.

"See you at ten," Sam tells her, as King jumps and barks, following the two cars out.

Back inside the cabin, Sam chooses three books from his grandfather's collection and sits with pen and paper handy at the desk, reading and taking notes under the light of the Coleman lantern. After midnight, Sam yawns. He finishes writing the sentence and crawls under the covers.

Fifteen

Arriving at Francinea's home, Sam puts King in her fenced backyard and enters through the patio door. Fran greets him with a warm hug. "Good morning. I've got great news for you. Mark and Susan will be here for our wedding. Remember that lady that's been harassing me about letting her husband die. She called. She begged me for forgiveness. So, I invited her to our wedding."

"Good. I heard that Pastor Thomas had been ministering to her." Samuel says. "I called the sheriff, and he offered to find the right size and type of tent we'll need. Now, how about this idea. Since I don't have a best man, King will be at my side when Meredith escorts you to the front. He'll be holding the ring in his jaws."

"What? In his mouth."

"No! I did not mean in his mouth. It'll be on a string tied onto his collar."

"You can pick from a half-dozen guys to be your best man. The sheriff or Gene would do it. Hmm? Well, that will certainly be a first." Fran says. "Let's go. In my car."

Arriving at the church, Pastor Thomas greets them at the entrance. "Sam, are you ready? I'll call you up after our worship time. You'll have five minutes."

"I guess so."

"Guess so? Yes or no? Sam, do you really want to do this?" Pastor Thomas asks again.

"He's always ready," Fran tells the pastor.

"Yeah, but after a few words, you may wish you had not asked me."

"I'm confident that won't be necessary."

George escorts Sam and Fran to the front row. After the musical worship, Pastor Thomas takes the stage.

"Good morning. Before I start my sermonizing, I have invited a loyal and benevolent good hardy friend to provide us with a short update. Let's all welcome Samuel Guardyall. Sam, come on up."

The congregation bursts into applause.

"Thank you," Sam says after he reclines in a camp chair next to the podium. Now, you may want to take back that generous welcome after a few minutes of my wonderings about this upcoming holiday of welcoming Santa Claus and reindeer landing on our roofs. Ah, what a joy we get watching the kiddies excitedly tear into their gifts. Where did this tradition come from? And why?

"Did Matthew, Mark, Luke, or John mention anything about Santa Claus? Paul? Sometime in the past, our secular tradition changed Saint Nicholas into that old white-bearded guy who plans his trip from the frozen north pole to bring presents to children. Hey, Dasher, Prancer, and Dancer. Giddy-up! Let's go! We've got work to do. Now, that guy was a miracle worker, somehow stopping at every home, squeezing down chimneys with a bag full of toys. And dad was glad as the insides of the chimney got cleaned. But, somehow very little dust from that squeeze. And before the next chimney descent, that bag was miraculously filled with the toys the kiddies wanted.

"How about the tree decorations? The mistletoe? The stockings? Where and when did those come from? You may have already researched that on the internet of everything. How about the songs we sing." Sam starts singing: *'It was the night before Christmas and all through the house, not a creature was stirring, not even a mouse'*. Oh, there had to be mice in those days, so Joesph may have put stockings on the tent supports to keep the mice from seeking comfort in Mary's socks. Oh? Did Mary even wear socks?

"How about the Happy Holiday cards you send? Oh, forget that as now we email those greetings."

Sam points to the trees on the sides of the podium.

"Oh, we couldn't have Christmas without a beautifully decorated pine tree with a star on top with strings of lights, tinsels, and hundreds of decorated balls carefully placed. And now, there are acres and acres of land devoted to growing pine trees.

"Many of these traditions started after the great wars ended, and when the military guys gladly returned home.

"Back in those Roman days, it was not recorded what day and hour Jesus was born listing his weight and length. Has anyone found his birth certificate? Did they get a new calendar every year? The Romans honored the pagan god Saturn from December 17th to the 25th. But our current calendar, the Gregorian was not instituted until 1582, with one day added every fourth year.

"Ah, does it really matter whether Jesus was born on December twenty-fifth or the nineteenth? Nope! What does matter, but what we don't think about it much, is how secular and, yes, pagan traditions have infiltrated the holiday. We've embraced those secular traditions. Remove them and there would be no Christmas shopping.

"You may have wondered why I'm sitting on this camp chair instead of standing behind the pulpit. Look at this chair. It has a nice comfy vinyl fabric supported by three wire posts on each corner, plus a back to lean on. I've enjoyed many hours of reclining on this chair by the stream, where I get a rabbit's view of the forest, lake, and the snowy mountains off in the distance.

"Look at the details of this chair." Sam points to the support posts. "One day, while relaxed on this chair, its framework got my attention. On each of the four corners supporting the seat, there are three posts, one, straight up on each corner, and two supporting the sides." He points down to the support posts on his right. "Without these vital supports, it wouldn't support me. Three posts? Why three on all four corners? Couldn't one or two be good enough, I thought. Then the Trinity came to mind. The Father, as the center support, with the Son and Holy Spirit alongside, provides me a safe place to relax. I looked at this chair and the way it's put together demonstrated the life, the story of Jesus as the support for this time that we celebrate Christmas. Yes, think of that. Without the birth of Jesus, there'd be no Christmas, just a normal month. No Santa. No gifts. No trees. None of that stuff.

"He was just one of the millions of babies. But this one was different from his first breath. The angel informed Mary that her son to be would be amazing. The angel also told Joesph, her husband to be not to worry. Shepherds were notified, left their flock, and found Mary with the baby in a manager. Three wise men from afar followed a star to see this baby who would become the new king and savior.

"And, in His way, the Father's way that boy did.

"As in the beginning, human life has been seized by, hampered by, and demonized by our arch-enemy, Satan, the god of this world, our spiritual enemy. All those secular traditions masking the birth of Our Savior have come from the master of evil where no truth is found. Santa Claus and all that guy does, our tree decorations, our gifts to the kids and each other, the stockings hung, are all secular traditions that pushed the real meaning of Christmas into the background. And because of our love of enjoyment, we don't see it as demonic, but fun, and yes, exciting.

"If we fought against all that and did not embrace these traditions, we'd get no extra days off work. The kiddies would be in school. December would be just an average month after our Thanksgiving celebration.

"The birth of Jesus is our time to celebrate, give thanks, rest, and enjoy our fellowship with the Lord of All, empowered by the Holy Spirit and enabled by the Great I Am.

"Santa Claus comes and goes, but the birth of Jesus, the messiah, and what that means is, and has been with us every day, every moment for two thousand years. Yes, Santa comes and goes, but Jesus never goes. He's always here."

Samuel pauses, takes a deep breath, looks and nods at the pastor.

"That's it."

Pastor Thomas steps on the stage. "Thank you, Sam. Now folks, let's stand and show our appreciation."

They all stand, clap, and cheer.

"Thank you, Sam. Yes, the day we celebrate the birth of our Lord is just two days away. Sam related that he'd like Christmas to pass quickly to bring on the New Year."

He signals to Francinea, "come on up."

She is helped onto the stage to stand alongside Samuel.

"Why would anyone want Christmas to end quickly?" Pastor Thomas continues. "On New Year's Eve, Sam said he'll be watching the fireworks with extra joy. Because, well, in the first day of next year, I am honored to lead Francinea and Sam in those marriage vows in a big tent next to his ancient cabin.

The audience explodes in applause. They stand and shout their glee.

"You are all welcome to attend this ceremony. Bring a cushion and dress warmly as the tent may not be like it is here in the comfort of our heated church and homes. And now, a short sermon."

Sam and Francinea return to their seats in the first row.

"As Sam said, in two days, we will celebrate the birth of our Lord, Jesus of Nazareth, the Son of God, the Almighty, the great I Am, the Creator of this universe, the stars, this lonely one of a kind planet that has an atmosphere enabling life to thrive. Here we are breathing this air into our lungs, pumping blood to our bodies, and this amazing organ under our hair and scalp. One part of our being is not physical: our soul. It's that soul of yours that connects to the Lord. And, it's that soul of yours that will enjoy the eternity of Heaven.

"Stand, and let's read about this miraculous birth. Open your Bibles, first to Matthew 1:18. We'll read that and then go to Luke 1:26"

"That's all for today. Lunch will be served in the community center in a half-hour, so greet one another, get your kiddies ready and grab a seat. Thank you, and God bless you each and every day."

On their way, Sam takes a second look at a couple standing by the doorway.

"Wanda, is that you?"

"Yes, boss, it's me." Wanda answers. She throws her arms around Sam's neck. Their hug is released, and Sam grabs the hand of her husband, Herbert.

"Wow! How's everything back there?" Looking at Herbert, Sam continues, "So, another skiing vacation. I'm so glad you stopped here, as I got great news for you. He turns to Fran. "Fran, honey, these two were friends of mine back in Shelbyville. Wanda was my secretary. Herbert and I played a little golf together. But, I never did any skiing with him."

Fran greets and hugs Wanda and her husband. "Good to meet you, and I'm sure Sam is delighted. If you are in the area on New Years Day, you're welcome to come to our wedding."

"I read the announcement in the Johnsonville times," Wanda says. "Here we are. We decided to spend a day here before heading west. Sam, I tried to keep up to date with this adventure of yours. It's been a chore. It's like you totally forgot about us. No letters. No postcards. No calls. No messages. No Facebook chats. I discovered Joyce Ripper on Facebook, and she has posted several items about this dude in a log cabin."

"Joyce?" Sam replies. "The lady at the laundromat?"

"Yes, Wanda replies. "She has updated me some about this adventure. Your dog getting sprayed. Your stops at the diner. She also connected us with a kid who could and would send a drone over your cabin. We watched you once, almost tipping the boat over after you caught a fish."

"No kidding? Oh, Wanda. Thank you so much for encouraging me the way you did to make the jump out here. God has blessed me beyond reason. How's the company doing? Those checks you've sent indicate it's doing rather well."

"Dennis has been great. He's now known as Samuel the Second. And, Kaki is about to jump ship to be on his own. We've got room for a rematch if you get tired of this anytime soon. Dennis would love to tell you what to do and when."

"That'll be the day. I've adjusted to the off-grid life. A few emergencies like shopping my leg open. That's how I met and fell in love with Fran here."

Fran the interjects. "Wanda and Herbert, I'd love to spend more time with you, but I've got an overnight eighteen-hour shift at the hospital, so I need some rest. They're understaffed as usual this time of the year. It's always like that during the holidays. The doctors and nurses with longevity get extra days off while we get to fill their shoes."

"Francinea, it's great to meet you, and we'll definitely be at the wedding," Herbert tells her.

"Yes, please do. Now you guys enjoy the skiing," Fran says. "I see Harry and Meredith coming. So, I'll catch a ride with them. Now, why don't you take your friends to view the insides of the cabin? Again, Wanda and Herbert, It's been great to meet you." Fran shakes their hands, kisses Sam, and waves at her daughter.

"Bye, honey. Get the rest. You never know when I might need your surgical skills again." Sam tells her.

Herbert and Wand follow Sam to the cabin. "This is it." He fires up the fireplace and stove, makes some coffee.

"How long will it take to bring it to a comfortable temperature?" Wanda asks. "And to see this in person is remarkable. Wow!"

"I spent a week in a similar cabin a few years ago on a skiing trip north of Yellowstone. It also had a typewriter such as this, but it was there only for decoration, You use this now?" Herbert says as he fingers the typewriter.

"Excuse me for a minute. I need to let King out of the barn," Sam says.

"Bring him in. See if he remembers me." She slides the pantry curtain aside and sees Sam's grandmother's hundreds of canned items. Herbert is scanning the numerous books on the shelves

"Wanda, dear, remember our trip to Springfield, Illinois when we stopped to visit the Lincoln Museum? This reminds me of that. The fireplace. The oil lamps. The books. Everything."

As Sam opens the door for King, the dog goes to sniff Herbert's legs, then sits and looks up. Herbert then rubs his neck. As Wanda leaves the pantry, King barks a few times and runs toward her. "Oh, King, you remember. Good doggie."

Sam pours them a cup of coffee as they sit in front of the warm fireplace. After about an hour of catching up on the news, Herbert suggests they should head to the hotel in Johnsonville. "It's getting late, and we got to get an early start in the morning for that five-hour trip to that ski resort."

"Yes, I guess we should. Sam, you're blessed, and we will be back for your wedding. Now, Merry Christmas."

Sam watches them leave as King runs alongside the car up the dirt road.

Back inside the cabin, Sam sits at the desk as an oil-burning lamp provides light, ready to focus his thoughts on paper.

My Cabin Life 22

Two days till Christmas, and nine days to the New Year. Yippee!

The surprise visit from Wanda and Herbert brightened the day. As my secretary for all those years, she managed to keep us afloat and concentrated on our projects. More than a secretary. She was an accountant too. Knew where every penny went. Screened our clients and calls. Her many suggestions on our designs from a woman's standpoint were invaluable and put the firm up there with the best.

And now some notes about this adventure into married life again, for both of us.

Sheriff Olsen updated us on the tent and other details. Gene said his class would install the tent, bring and place the chairs and the podium. It'll be ready a few days before. And, the weather forecast looks good, as that day is forecast as clear skies after a foot of snow supposedly falls three previous days.

As I told the pastor and, of course, Francinea, my new love, I wanted to skip all that Christmas stuff and get this new event in my life started. Fran did too.

Why wait then? Let's do it.

But oh, traditions get in the way. We're supposed to plan everything according to those rituals.

Did the old-timers plan weddings two, three, six months before the big day so the bride's parents could prepare their daughter for her new caretaker? What kind of preparations? How did Adam and Eve arrange the marriage of their kids?

Noah and his kids? How were those weddings performed between brothers and perhaps daughters-in-law. Did those ancients have these numerous things accepted by all that precedes a male and female union? No.

It's written that King Solomon had 700 wives and 300 concubines. Wow! When did he get time off to rule the country? Didn't the wives fight each other over who's next?

Throughout history, the female gender was considered her parents' property and then the property of her eventual husband. Yes, property to be bought or sold. Is that when the tradition of giving the bride's family a dowry came from? Buying the daughter for their son. The man owned his wife, and she was expected to remain in the home, cook, clean, tend to the kiddies, and keep herself available to his wants and needs.

He was allowed to have relations with other ladies, but if she did? Yikes!

The Greeks did it one way—the Romans another. The Mesopotamians did it their way. Jews, according to the law. Some of the traditions had matchmakers selecting two eligible from a list who wanted to get married and have children. Was it basically to please their parents, who thought the match was good. The man and lady met somewhere and discussed the plans. Did they have a choice?

Sorry son, but you must take her. This is how it works. This is how we do that.

But I've met someone else. Too bad. You cannot break our way of doing things.

And here we are. Two folks of middle-age who have lost their first love to a tragedy, now desiring the loving fellowship of each other.

Really, why must those traditions bind us? We're not teenagers or young adults doing this for the first time. A pastor could be present as a witness, as Fran and I get on our knees, say our vows, and that's it. Ceremony over, now get the marriage document through the courts.

Yeah, why not?

Here we go again. Submitting and following our societal ways of doing things. Anyway, we will be going traditional, with a few new ones.

This is what and how we will do it, adding my personal trademark, to which Fran has agreed.

"Yes," she said. "That will be a first."

Since my dog, King, has been my best addition to the sudden move into this log cabin to escape memories. He will be the best man standing with me as Fran will be escorted by her daughter Meredith to the tent in my grandfather's horse-drawn carriage.

Meredith then will lead her mother down the aisle to give her mother away. King will have the ring and give me away with a few barks.

As Pastor Thomas announces us as man and wife, King will point his nose straight up and give one of those long woooooo's wagging his tail. Oh, I've got some training to do.

After this, it's traditional to have a feast. Well, not here in the tent. Fran and I, wrapped in warm blankets riding in that horse-drawn carriage, will follow the sheriff. He will lead us, and the audience in their cars to the country club there in Johnsonville for a nice warm reception. One long line of cars honking as they slowly follow the speed of the horse.

After that reception, the guests will line up their cars and lead Fran and I back to the cabin.

Ya, Ha. Joy runneth over.

OH, I could go on and on about this new life of mine. After a few weeks of being here, the doubts and wonders pelleted my head. Why, oh why did I do it? The loneliness. The continual desire for human fellowship. The hardships of living the ways of Lincoln, of Columbus, of those countless millions living without our modern conveniences of electricity, temperature-controlled homes, plastic boxes of wi-fi connecting us to everywhere and anyone. Yet, I made it. I vowed that I would and could.

But, oh, the mysteries of it all. The Lord God of mysteries knew what I needed and provided a way that was a mystery to me. Why? At first sight of the letter, the pictures, the legal document willing me this cabin, I wondered why?

But Wanda emphatically said, "Yes! Do it."

I had never met my grandfather, and here he was bestowing on me the same life where he lived his entire ninety-four years. He was birthed right here in front of this fireplace. He never embraced our technology-driven life

A life without conveniences and comfort was a log cabin escape life for me. I did it one day at a time, and am now excited that I did. And now, eight months later, a new life of loving human fellowship awaits me on New Years Day.

    Yahoo!   Happy New Year!

Yes, the Lord led me beside these still waters.

The End.

Books previously published by Arnold Kropp

November 2012

Mark is a farmer and inventor living the good life with his wife Susan of 33 years. While building up the interest in their Halloween Festival on the farm, Mark gets disenchanted, then obsessed, and desires to leave all the comforts behind to follow a desire for freedom. After experiencing a peace that passes understanding, an unsuspected surprise disturbs their tranquility, forcing them to form new plans.

December 2013

Thoroughly enjoying the solitude of island life for six months, they are suddenly surprised as an old friend shows up with an additional 300 like-minded Americans. The extra people put demands upon them to organize and form a community. This sequel begins as the daily life of building a community continues as surprises from the mainland put them off guard. They are visited by the UN, shocked by Navy jets, surprised as a small group of Russians locate on the island. All they desired to do was to live peacefully, enjoying the close relationships of family and friends.

2017
The school bus. When did it start, how it has evolved, and why was it necessary?

2019
Just a Matter of Time is a Christian-based novel about a rural family dealing with governmental intrusions brought on by the technological advances over every area of life. What will the computerized world of technology be like in ten, twenty, thirty years? Follow this family of four dealing with the

Samuel assumed he was a Christian. A personal tragedy turns his life upside down. He accepts the offer from his late grandfather, sells his business and home to escape memories. He works at adjusting to life in an old log cabin surrounded by a national forest. A federal agency wants the cabin as a museum. He writes of the insights revealed in the wonders of our created nature and desires to share this new faith. His daily life is without human interactions, so he invites locals out for campfire chats. A high school principal turns down a request. A widow gets his attention.

About the Author.

Back in the days when Arnold was a kid growing up in south Chicago, he freely roamed the neighborhood after school. A public golf course was just two blocks away. He and his buddies ran across the four-lane busy Western avenue by running between an opening of the cars and trucks and then climb the fence to sled down the slopes in the winter snows. We knew the risks. No one got hurt.

After graduating HS, he went to a Christian College in Wisconsin, and before graduation, he turned the responsibility of his life over to the US Army. As a Morse Code Operator, he was transferred to Germany, joining a Long Range Recon Patrol. Driving a '49 Volkswagen into Berlin with a few friends, he got a personal look at the Brandenburg Gate being walled-off to keep those in the East from enjoying the freedoms of the West. He spent several days in Switzerland and a trip to Stockholm, Sweden, to visit his mother's cousin.

After his 1962 discharge, he moved to Atlanta, Ga, and returned to school. He signed up for a student exchange summer to live with a German family. for the ten week summer.

He returned to school, married a southern gal, and moved to Florida to start a retail management career, eventually relocating to Grand Rapids, Michigan. In 1979, he moved to Broken Arrow, Oklahoma, to attend a two-year Bible school.

After he retired from a career with the City of Tulsa, he drove a school bus part-time. Try that sometime. The retirement provided time to write. A hobby enjoyed throughout his life.

www.ingramcontent.com/pod-product-compliance
Lightning Source LLC
Chambersburg PA
CBHW042343300426
44109CB00049B/2762